MASKS AN[

MASKS AND FACES

The Life and Career of Harry Braham

Janet Muir

*To Margaret
Best Wishes
from
[signature]*

CHAPLIN BOOKS

www.chaplinbooks.co.uk

Copyright © Janet Muir

First published in 2014 by Chaplin Books

ISBN 978-1909-183-50-6

All rights reserved. No part of this publication may be reproduced, stored in any retrieval system or transmitted in any form or by any means, electronic, mechanical, photocopying, recording or otherwise, without the prior written permission of the copyright holder for which application should be addressed in the first instance to the publishers. No liability shall be attached to the author, the copyright holder or the publishers for loss or damage of any nature suffered as a result of the reliance on the reproduction of any of the contents of this publication or any errors or omissions in the contents.

A CIP catalogue record for this book
is available from The British Library

Design by Michael Walsh at The Better Book Company

Printed by Imprint Digital

Chaplin Books
1 Eliza Place
Gosport PO12 4UN
Tel: 023 9252 9020
www.chaplinbooks.co.uk

CONTENTS

Introduction i
Prologue v
Chapter One: Hard Times in the Rookery 1
Chapter Two: The Royal Christy Minstrels 10
Chapter Three: Pulling Mugs in the Music Hall 15
Chapter Four: Down Under 21
Chapter Five: When Harry Met Lizzie 26
Chapter Six: A Venture into Burlesque 41
Chapter Seven: Aloha Harry 49
Chapter Eight: Yankee Doodle Harry 52
Chapter Nine: Homecoming 60
Chapter Ten: Heartbreak 66
Chapter Eleven: Going Solo 71
Chapter Twelve: Harry Turns Legit 84
Chapter Thirteen: Peril at Sea 96
Chapter Fourteen: Breaking Away 103
Chapter Fifteen: Citizen Braham 109
Chapter Sixteen: Moving Pictures 118
Chapter Seventeen: The Final Curtain 127
Afterword 128
Appendices:
Harry Braham's Articles on the Film Industry 131
A Literary Curiosity 139
Music Halls at which Harry Braham Appeared 141
Sources 158
Acknowledgements 160
Index 161

To my husband Hugh, with thanks for his love, support, help and encouragement; and in loving memory of my mother Joan Anderson (neé Braham) 12 Oct 1925 – 15 Jan 2014

INTRODUCTION

The building on the Trongate in Glasgow was dilapidated. Its blue paint was flaking off and trees were growing through the windows. I knew nothing of its history but, as soon as I stepped inside the door, I had the most overpowering sense of déjà vu: the feeling which I'd had for so long of not belonging, of restlessness and rootlessness, just evaporated. It shocked me with its power. What was this building? What was its history? And, more importantly, why had it had such an effect on me? What I found out was to change my life.

I was born in 1963 and, by the time my father left the army in 1970, I had lived in England, Singapore and Germany. I was used to moving around: we settled in Hampshire for five years but another job move meant travelling to the Highlands of Scotland and then a final move to Glasgow in 1982. This rather fractured upbringing left me lacking in confidence and with a pervasive feeling of rootlessness.

It was when I was working for the Civil Service that I met Hugh, who was to become my husband. We were the oddballs of the office, preferring old-time interests like history and theatre rather than the usual entertainment of pubs and football which most of my colleagues seemed to prefer. Hugh made me laugh, cracking jokes and doing impressions of famous performers. Through our interest in old buildings, we went on a holiday tour of the Beamish Museum in County Durham which had recreated Victorian streets and shops, and this increased my fascination with the era. When, in 1998, we saw an article in the local paper about a Glasgow hall called the Britannia Panopticon and the campaign to save it, we were quick to contact the organiser, Judith Bowers, to arrange a personal tour.

The building was originally used as a blacking factory and spirits' dealers. In 1854 the architects Gildard and MacFarlane were commissioned to design it as a department store with a beautiful façade, inspired by Alexander 'Greek' Thomson, but they soon realised that they had made a mistake. Though it was near the Merchant City where the rich tobacco lords had their businesses, the well-off were moving to the west end of the city, which was growing more affluent with better accommodation and transportation. The East End had now become one of the most poverty-stricken areas and the street contained a number of brothels and pubs. Gildard and MacFarlane therefore altered their design to enable the building to become a place of entertainment for the poor. It was built in 1857 and opened in December 1859 as the Britannia Music Hall, with John Brand as its first manager.

The building changed ownership a number of times, with its last, the eccentric Yorkshireman Albert Ernest Pickard (known as AE Pickard Unlimited) – taking it over in 1906. It was Pickard who made the hall a multi-faceted entertainment venue with a freak show, waxworks, carnival and zoo together with a new invention – the cinematograph, which had been introduced by the previous managers, Arthur Hubner and William Kean, in 1896. He renamed the building the Britannia and Grand Panopticon. When he introduced amateur nights at the music hall performances, a young Stan Laurel made his debut at the age of 16. The local populace, however, could not pronounce Panopticon and so they named it affectionately the 'pots and pans'.

When the cinematograph became more popular, the Panopticon was renamed the Tron Cinema, showing the latest films, but Glasgow was now building plush new picture palaces and Pickard, though immensely rich (he owned many of Glasgow's tenements) did not want to use his money to update the hall, which was looking tired. Instead, he sold the building in 1938 to the tailors Weaver to Wearer, and a false ceiling was put up below the balcony area, which was left to deteriorate. Over the next 60 years a number of owners used the building as a shop, with the main body of the hall stripped away and used as a storage facility.

A campaign had now begun to conserve it – and we were keen to become involved. In 2004, at an open day, there was a visitors' book which had a space for volunteering. But what skills could we offer? Hugh was good at monologues, so he put that. I didn't know what to put, so in the end I wrote 'backstage help'. It wasn't until 2005 that we finally joined the volunteer team. We started taking part in shows and preparations for 'open doors' weekends which were very busy: every time I went into the hall even though it was bitterly cold, I had a warm safe feeling, I no longer questioned why; I just enjoyed the feeling.

In 2010, I was speaking to one of our friends in the hall in casual conversation about the TV programme 'Who Do You Think You Are' and we got chatting about our ancestors. I mentioned a story I had heard during my childhood about a relative who was a comedian and his brother – my great-great-grandfather – who had been an acrobat. I was asked if either of them had appeared at the Britannia: it was not something I'd ever thought about, but now – with the internet available for researching genealogy – I decided to find out.

With some trepidation, I entered their names on a search engine. I had no luck at all with my great-great-grandfather's name, but when I entered his brother's name, hundreds of articles were listed. I was amazed. I took out a subscription to access the archives of *The Era*, the professional magazine for music hall performers at the time. This time I had more luck with my great-great-grandfather's name, but once again it was my great-great-uncle whose name kept coming up. I started reading some of the articles about him and stumbled upon one about him appearing at the Britannia. My heart started beating fast as I read – I felt faint and the colour drained from my face. Was this the reason I had been so drawn to the building after having lived in so many places? Was this the reason for that powerful feeling the first time I entered and the warm feeling I continued to have? Was it fate, or just coincidence?

All I did know was that I felt a gratitude to this man I had never known, and who I had heard so little about, but who had, by some means, turned my life around. I determined to pay tribute to him.

His name was Harry Braham, and this is his story.

Janet Muir
Glasgow, March 2014

The 'City of Richmond'

PROLOGUE

Everyone on deck! All hands on deck! Fire! Fire! Bring the hose quick! As the steamship lurched in the heavy seas, Harry grabbed what clothes he could; coughing and with his eyes smarting from the smoke, he struggled with the other terrified passengers to climb the ladders. On deck, with the rain lashing down and the wind howling, he gripped the rails of the ship tightly, trying to stay upright. With horror he saw the flames leaping high in the hold and he thought his time had come.

CHAPTER ONE
Hard Times in the Rookery

London 1848. Seven Dials was part of the notorious rookery of St Giles, a place where thieves abounded, prostitutes lured men to ply their trade then rob them, bare-foot filthy urchins begged for scraps of food, and drunks staggered out of the many pubs. Murders went unnoticed, for the Peelers – fearing for their lives – did not venture there.

The stench was appalling with cesspits in the streets, dead animals left to rot, and horse-manure lying all around. Pigs, cattle and sheep were beaten as they were led to Smithfield Market, with the bloodied slaughterhouses creating their own peculiar smells. The sulphur from gas lighting and smoke from coal fires produced dense, yellow, choking, pea-soup fogs. Rubbish was everywhere and scavenging rats ran through the dark alleyways. The smell was made worse with overflowing sewage pouring directly into the River Thames from the inadequate sewers. Flies swarmed over the putrid matter, the miasma being carried throughout the city. Seven Dials became home to Irish immigrants who had fled the potato famine only to find impoverishment in the heart of the city. It became known as 'The Holy Land'.

Amid this pestilence it didn't take long for a cholera epidemic to happen. Thousands of people died in London every day, their only source of water the Thames. Typhus-carrying lice flourished among the unwashed mass of poverty-stricken people, creating another epidemic. Some families were wiped out; in others, husbands mourned the loss of their wives, and new orphans cried piteously. Smallpox was rife and its survivors – some hideously scarred and many blind – were feared and pitied in turn.

Yet despite the desolation and despair there was still hope, for on Saturday 11 November bells could be heard ringing from the nearby St Martin in the Fields parish church: a wedding was taking place.

As Nathaniel Henry Braham and Susan Dorothy Frost left the church as man and wife on that cold winter day, everything looked just the same as when they'd gone in – opposite was the newly built National Gallery, with the gruesome workhouse behind. Trafalgar Square, with Nelson's Column only half-finished, though busy with people and a cacophony of noise from the carriages darting here and there, still seemed eerily peaceful after the Chartist Riots in March; and just beyond the workhouse they could hear the soldiers of St George's Barracks parading. But now the malodorous air surrounding them seemed insignificant; the muck where they carefully trod in their 'Sunday best' did not seem so fetid. They had sacrificed so much for this day – this was their reality now and whatever lay ahead, they would face together.

Nathaniel was Jewish, from a fairly well-off family, but Susan was a miller's daughter and an Anglican. This clash of cultures, not only of religion but of class, resulted in conflict and animosity within Nathaniel's family and he had been told that to marry her would be to risk ex-communication from the faith and estrangement from his family. He had made his decision and, although he did not renounce his faith, he found he was ostracised: he hoped that his family would come round eventually. This trauma affected the rest of his life, but his love for Susan did not diminish.

He had trained as an artist, dependent on commissions, but work was difficult to come by and they had little money. He managed to rent a room for himself and Susan in the Seven Dials on the corner of Upper St Martin's Lane, in West Street, next to John Moore's betting shop and every day they passed the wretched souls lining up to be admitted to the workhouse, a grim reminder of life at its most degrading. Until now, Nathaniel had never experienced destitution and the sights, sounds and smells were a shock to his senses. Most of the people he came into contact with had no hope and no means of leaving the hovels they called home. Nathaniel, however, was an educated man who had known a life outside the slums and he vowed that he would do all he could to restore the wealth he had previously known and to protect his new family from the workhouse, particularly as Susan was now pregnant.

Pregnancy and childbirth were hazardous, mortality rates high, and Nathaniel was afraid for his wife's safety and that of his unborn child. They were both relieved and delighted when she delivered a healthy son on 13 September 1850. They named the baby Henry Nathaniel after his father, but within the family he was known as Harry.

Harry was four months old in January 1851 when his parents were awoken by shouts and screams close to their small room in West Street. The sounds of drunken noise and fighting were now familiar to them but this was different; they also smelt smoke. Harry started crying. While Susan soothed him, Nathaniel hurriedly dressed and went to investigate the commotion. He saw the flames lighting up the sky, the acrid smell of the smoke from another burning building all too recognisable, but this time he could see it was one of the largest buildings in St Martin's Lane, the three-storey pub the Coach and Horses Tavern, known all around the area for being owned by Benjamin Caunt, the famous six-foot-two-inch, eighteen stone, heavyweight champion bare-knuckle fighter. Nathaniel had seen the giant of a man many times and would have known his nicknames of 'The Torkard Giant' or 'Big Ben'.

Now, he saw Caunt's wife, who had escaped through the skylight with one of her sons; she was screaming that their two other children – Cornelius and Martha – were inside trapped by the blaze. The firemen came within minutes, their horses racing along the cobbled streets. The building was now an inferno, crumbling in a heap of ashes and fallen timber. The charred remains of the children, aged six and eight, were found together with a servant amid the smouldering wreck later that day.

The tragedy was talked about for weeks, the burnt-out shell a reminder of the heartbreak. Everyone wondered why it had happened, but the cause at the inquest was found to be simple – a candle had caught a piece of fabric.

Nathaniel and Susan's sympathy for the family was tempered by their own daily struggle to survive. Their circumstances worsened a short time later when they were told by their landlord that he needed their room, and they would have to leave. By chance a friend from the barracks, Captain Edward Wilson, was looking for lodgings and he agreed to help out with the rent. They moved their meagre possessions a few hundred yards away to 17 Upper St Martin's Lane above a coffee house.

Later that year Susan announced she was expecting another baby. The rookery of St Giles – which stretched from Great Russell Street, Charing Cross Road and Shaftesbury Avenue to Tottenham Court Road and Oxford Street – was being demolished to make way for New Oxford Street. No new housing was built. Nathaniel, Susan with their infant son, and many other families were evicted into more overcrowded slums. They gathered what they could and were forced to move south of the river, nearer the stinking Thames. They rented a room in Royal Street, Lambeth, and it was here on 30 April 1852 that their second son was born. They registered his birth as Nathaniel but he was known in the family as Charles to avoid confusion with his father.

Instead of the wealth Nathaniel craved, their quality of life was deteriorating. Seven Dials was a violent place, but Lambeth was worse: the Bethlehem Lunatic Asylum was nearby and an horrific murder was committed the same month Charles was born when, in a moment of madness, a newly released patient named Thomas Wheeler decapitated his mother Elizabeth on the kitchen table Only three months later, a decorator Henry Simmonds was charged with the rape of a 16-year-old in the same street they lived in.

Nathaniel was finding it increasingly difficult to pay the rent and with Susan pregnant again, they fled overnight, this time to St Pancras. Another slum area, it was surrounded by overcrowded cemeteries, with decomposing bodies turning the earth to a putrefying liquid. Nathaniel somehow was able to get more work, and they rented a room where their last child, another son, was born on 31 March 1854. They named him Edwin.

In 1858, Harry was seven and – having known nothing else – would have been accustomed to the stinking river, but the heat of that summer was unusual and now the whole of London complained at the overpowering stench. Going outside, people used handkerchiefs soaked in perfume to stop them gagging, but the foul smell lingered on clothing which made it impossible to ignore. Together with the thick fogs it made daily life intolerable. Cholera was endemic and the accepted theory was that it was caused by bad air. Even in the more affluent areas, people were afraid for their lives. When the rain came, it was a relief – and much of the stench dissipated.

The Houses of Parliament, because of its situation on the bank of the Thames, was much affected by what became known as The Big Stink. Politicians used chloride of lime to cover the windows, and considered evacuating to Hampton Court. They agreed something had to be done to solve this miasma, so they employed Joseph Bazalgette, an engineer, to design an underground sewer system to "enclose the smell". The sewers would not be completed until 1875, but in the meantime their construction disrupted the whole of London as tunnels were built and houses destroyed. Clearing the Thames of faecal matter meant that many of the water-borne diseases disappeared, but it was many years before it was finally accepted that polluted water was to blame.

So far, Nathaniel had not been able to give his family the kind of life he had wanted to, and he realised that being a full-time artist was not going to provide enough money. He had never known any other occupation, and had lurched from relative stability to poverty. He decided to try working as a turf accountant. His upbringing meant he was well-educated, and he was good with figures; horseracing was the most popular sport in the UK at the time and when he had lived in West Street the bookmaker at the corner of the street was one of the most profitable occupations. He found he had a talent for this and, with any income which he could get from occasional art-work, they were at last able to move out of the slums to slightly better accommodation in Hunter Street, just off Brunswick Square near the Foundling Hospital.

By 1861, thanks to his hard work, their lives improved even more and they were able to take up residence at Lanark Villas in Paddington, where they had a servant, and two boarders. Nathaniel had come a long way from the squalor of St Martin's Lane.

On 22 June the family would have watched as the London sky turned different shades of red and orange; explosions could be heard far and wide, and a massive plume of smoke could be seen from miles around. Warehouses holding hemp, tallow, cotton and oil in Tooley Street near London Bridge had caught fire. As the conflagration swept through building after building, spilling fat into the Thames, thousands of spectators came to watch, boats were hired and people started gathering the tallow: four died when one caught fire. The Edinburgh-born Chief Fire Officer James Braidwood, who had instigated many fire-fighting methods and was one of the first on the scene, was killed when a wall fell on him – his body could not be recovered for three days. The fire burned for two weeks, and when Braidwood's funeral took place on 29 June the number of people who came to pay their respects rivalled that of a monarch's funeral. Every bell apart from St Paul's tolled and shops closed their doors in honour of his extreme bravery and sacrifice. The fire service, which was owned by insurance companies threatened to close fire stations unless the Government took over – which it did in 1865, starting the London Fire Brigade.

Nathaniel, stressed from overwork, started drinking heavily, and on a trip to Sheffield in 1862 accused a man of stealing a £20 diamond ring. He was – as he admitted – very drunk at the time, having gone from bar to bar, and insensible when he got to his lodging; but nevertheless, the man was remanded in custody.

The family now had a good standard of living, and the boys were having private tuition. Nathaniel, however, was still determined to prosper and their next house, in Stanley Street, Pimlico, was in an upmarket neighbourhood. As they had a servant, and Nathaniel had a good educational background, the Brahams now considered themselves to be middle class and mixed with lawyers and accountants, but Nathaniel's drinking and some bad business deals meant that by the end of the year they were in serious financial difficulties. After defaulting on the rent, Nathaniel filed for bankruptcy on 31 March 1863.

Remembering his vow in St Martin's Lane, he was humiliated; how could he have let this happen? This could have led to his family being ripped apart: the thought of poverty again, and possibly even the workhouse, petrified him and he decided that he would never again put his family through this. He gave up being an artist: it had been taking up too much time for little reward, but the bookmaking business in general was still thriving, and he gave up drinking. With Susan's support he managed to regain what he had lost. Nathaniel also became a Freemason, believing that its moral ethics would help him.

As a Mason, he mingled with many of the rich men of the day. He enjoyed debating, but one thing annoyed him more than anything else: the majority of the people did not have the right to vote. This meant that the deprivation they suffered would never end. Laws were made by the aristocracy and property owners, many of whom had little time for the poor, who he empathised with having endured poverty for so many years. But politics, as well as religion, were the only subjects banned at meetings. Giving to charity was one of the Masons' ethics and he gave where he could, but he wanted to do more.

Dissent had been steadily growing among working men to have electoral rights. A group of men led by ex-Chartist John Bedford Leno formed The Reform League in 1865 and they started demonstrating to force Government to give them the vote. At first the marches were violent, but when they began encouraging middle-class men to join their cause to give them more power, they became peaceful. Nathaniel decided to join the League, becoming part of the biggest meeting in its history on 30 July 1866 at the Agricultural Hall in Islington. The various demonstrations held around the country culminated in the Reform Act of 1867, which saw working-class men given the right to vote for the first time. Women had no voting rights at all, of course, something that would not change for another 50 years.

The family was growing up, and the boys were each developing their own personalities. Harry was an outgoing, stubborn lad and loved to be the centre of attention; though intelligent, he had no interest in academic learning. This infuriated his father who had fought so hard for his boys' education. As Harry's voice broke, he found he was a good singer with a talent for mimicry and loved to make people laugh by pulling funny faces. He argued with his father: he wanted to be on the stage, but Nathaniel was very much against it. It was not the sort of lowly occupation Nathaniel had envisaged for his eldest son. Charles was a good student and excelled at French. He was also good at mathematics, and Nathaniel had high hopes that he would be a lawyer or specialist in some field. Edwin was able to read and write, but he struggled, and as he grew up his parents came to realise he would never be able to live by himself.

Although Nathaniel was against young Harry going on the stage, his mother took a different view. When the family's circumstances improved back in 1861, she had some leisure for the first time and sang a few seasons at Covent Garden Opera House with the Pyne and Harrison Opera Company. When the family became bankrupt, she had to give up her singing. Nathaniel, anxious to appear a middle-class gentleman, may not entirely have approved of her singing, though opera and theatre were considered respectable as they were the reserve of the middle and upper classes. For working-class men the only entertainment on offer was the rowdy supper room or bar with bawdy singers, which provided some relief from the rigours of daily life, but Nathaniel would not have seen this as a fit place for his son to work. Then a new 'respectable' entertainment came over from America that would be a path towards Harry's future career – minstrels.

In the 1830s groups of minstrels had toured the United States, with the first well-known 'blackface' minstrel being Thomas Dartmouth Rice with his song and dance 'Jump Jim Crow', but the shows had no distinct structure. By the 1850s Edwin Pearce Christy (1815-1862) had devised a proper show which consisted of three parts: in the first, a troupe would dance in costume to a rousing tune and the interlocutor or chairman would say "Gentlemen be seated". On one side of him would be a man with a tambourine – called the 'tambo' – and on the other side, a man with castanets or 'bones'. These 'endmen' would joke with the interlocutor whose job it was to introduce the acts, which would usually consist of singing and dancing, sometimes with a solo tenor singing a slow number. The second act was called the olio and was a variety show, with acrobats, dancing and musical instruments – one of the endmen would tell jokes or puns while moving about like a clown, and would often send up current issues of the day. The third act was usually a burlesque, (a parody of a well-known play) or slapstick humour.

These troupes came to be called The Christy Minstrels. The men (mainly white men, but there were black minstrels too) wore brightly coloured costumes and used burnt cork to blacken their faces, taking inspiration for their music and humour from the slave population. African Americans made up a very large part of their audience.

When the minstrels came to the UK after Christy's death, only some of the original troupe remained and they then split into four different troupes, all calling themselves a variation of the 'Christys' and any minstrel group thereafter was associated with that name.

Minstrelsy was the first entertainment to appeal to all classes and became hugely popular with everyone from royalty to the ordinary people in the street. Harry had his uncle Fred to thank for his introduction to minstrelsy.

CHAPTER TWO
The Royal Christy Minstrels

Uncle Fred Burgess was married to Susan's sister, Emma. Born in London, he became a minstrel with the Christy Minstrels and had worked his way up to manage a troupe. He also managed other clients, one of whom was William Makepeace Thackeray, author of *Vanity Fair*, whose public lecture tour about the first four Hanoverian monarchs, 'The Four Georges' was managed by Fred.

Fred Burgess, who started his career with the Christy Minstrels

Fred formed a partnership with an American minstrel, George Washington 'Pony' Moore, and they decided to find a base for the minstrels rather than go on tour.

The St James' Hall at the corner of Regent Street and Vine Street at Piccadilly was a fine hall with a Gothic façade, decorated in Florentine design imitating the Alhambra in Leicester Square. With one main hall able to hold 2,000 people, two smaller halls and two restaurants, it was the perfect venue, and they took out a permanent lease on one of the smaller rooms in 1865. As Moore was the more outgoing of the two, he attended to the entertainment side and Burgess the managerial. The troupe – initially called the Christy Minstrels before being renamed the Moore and Burgess Minstrels – was phenomenally successful and was in residence at the hall for over 30 years.

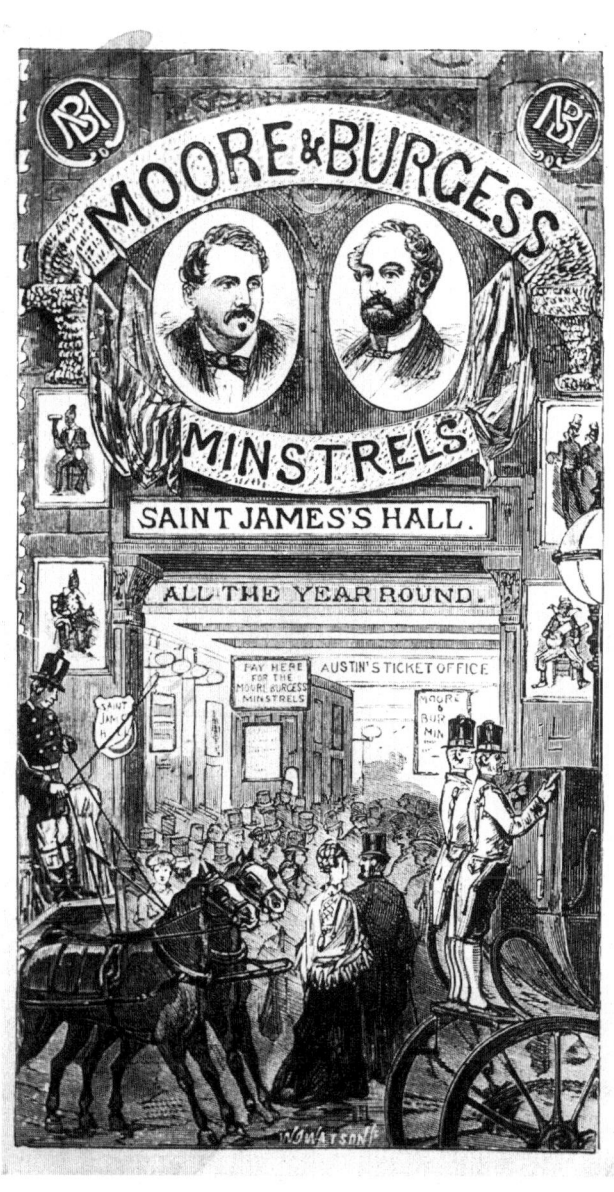

Moore and Burgess Minstrels, managed by Fred Burgess, was in residence at the St James' Hall for over 30 years

Fred was to become a very wealthy man and owner of a magnificent mansion set in 21 acres of land in Finchley.

In these early days, however, Fred and Emma lived with their children, Florence and Washington, in Bridges Street near the Theatre Royal, Drury Lane. There was speculation that Fred and George Moore were not on friendly terms, but there is no evidence for this: indeed, later, Fred and George lived only doors away from each other in Chelsea and it is likely that Fred named his son Washington after him. At family gatherings, when he was about 11, Harry would make everyone laugh at his antics and his natural flair for comedy flourished. He was fascinated by his uncle's stories, and wanted to know all about the minstrels and America: it sounded an exciting life, far better than being a lawyer (which is what his father wanted him to be) and he dreamt of going to America someday.

As often as he could, Harry visited St James' Hall and the sight of the gaily coloured minstrels singing and dancing made him more determined than ever to go on the stage. He continually rowed with his father about this. Nathaniel was furious: he himself had had to give up being an artist in order to give Harry the standard of life he had now. He was conscious that, for every success, there were hundreds of other actors destitute and he couldn't bear the thought of Harry becoming one of them. Susan, as a singer herself, knew the pull of the stage, and was torn between that, her husband's rage and her own genuine concern. Finally Harry confronted his father and in no uncertain terms told him that if he could not go on the stage with his permission, he would go on without it and would leave the family forever.

Susan pleaded with Nathaniel to go and see Fred, reminding him that – although under different circumstances – it was a family feud which had caused him to lose touch with his own family, and that Fred could possibly help solve this crisis. Perhaps Fred could employ Harry and thus keep him close to the family? Nathaniel reluctantly acknowledged that she was right: he recognised Harry's stubbornness as one of his own characteristics, he still missed his estranged family, and the thought of losing his son as well tormented him. Fred told Nathaniel and Susan he would employ Harry on a trial basis.

Harry proved to be a hard worker. His excellent memory meant that he quickly learnt the songs and dances of the show, and he acquired the art of blackening his face with burnt cork. He soon became part of the minstrel chorus in the St James' Hall.

It was the best place to learn his craft, as it was also home to the Philharmonic Society and second only to the Crystal Palace, which was the foremost venue for events, having been built for the Great Exhibition in 1851. He got the chance to see famous composers, conductors and musicians including Grieg, Tchaikovsky, Sir Arthur Sullivan, Charles Gounod, Dvorak, and Saint-Saens, all of whom played there. The minstrels were situated below the main hall, and their spectacular shows proved so popular that occasionally the upper classes who flocked to see the classical musicians were enticed into the hall if they felt the music was becoming monotonous.

The St James' Hall also played host to other entertainments such as lectures and talks and it was there that Charles Dickens gave a series of 12 readings, making his final one on 15 March 1870, before his death in June that year. Harry would undoubtedly have seen Dickens, who was well-known for performing his stories during his talks: many of Dickens' characters were to inspire Harry's act as he later developed his solo career.

Although Harry was content to stay for the trial period, and realised his uncle's troupe was a resident one, he was also impatient and wanted to travel. As soon as he could, he got work with another touring company of Christy Minstrels which were managed by Wilsom and Montague. In September 1868, when he was 18, Harry finished up a series of concerts in Aberdeen with them and then they all went down to Newcastle-upon-Tyne. A few days later a telegram was received and there was great excitement within the group when it was announced that Queen Victoria, who had heard about them when they were performing in Scotland, had commanded them to appear before her and her family at Balmoral on 16 October. Though it was 300 miles away, the full company of 20 performers packed up and headed back up north immediately. It was the first time a minstrel company had been asked to appear before royalty and it was a great honour. Harry was euphoric: he couldn't wait to tell his family because he could now prove to his father that acting wasn't so lowly!

As the troupe travelled up by train and then came through the estate by horse and carriage, the chatter and nerves must have been intense. The sight of the huge castle as they drew closer may have even stopped any talk at all. The professional troupe had performed hundreds of times before an audience, but how would they be received? This could make or break them. It would have been an exciting, but scary, time as they were led through to the ballroom by the liveried servants to await Her Majesty.

As the Queen came into the room, accompanied by many of her family including the royal household and high officials, Harry and the troupe bowed and began the show. They managed to get through without a hitch and then they sang, as a finale, the comic song *The Royal Wild Beast Show*, a tribute to the Manders Menagerie animal shows which were extremely popular around the country and which regularly appeared at the Tower of London

The Queen, widowed for seven years, had recently come out of self-imposed isolation, and the minstrels made her laugh. She asked for a couple of extra songs, and a few days later they were given permission to use 'Royal' as part of their name: the troupe became known as The Royal Christy Minstrels.

All the performers could hardly believe this had happened and it was difficult to return to performing in rather less exalted venues in the following days.

Harry enjoyed being part of the troupe, and soaked up the applause of the audience. What he really wanted, though, was to be centre stage. He was soon to get the chance – in the world of music hall.

CHAPTER THREE
Pulling Mugs in the Music Hall

Music hall, an offshoot of the bawdy supper rooms, had now become more acceptable as family entertainment, almost exclusively for the poor. Charles Morton (1819-1904), the man who became known as 'The Father of The Halls', had seen an opportunity to develop an entertainment for everyone, but for that to happen, singers and acts had to be 'cleaned up' from the bawdy supper saloons mainly geared to a male audience. He decided a new building was required and chose the site of the former Canterbury tavern at Westminster Bridge, not far from where the Braham family had lived in Lambeth. He named it the Canterbury Music Hall and it opened in 1852: when that burned down shortly afterwards, a bigger and better building was opened in 1854. It was Morton, a superb manager and impresario, who first coined the phrase 'music hall': his vision was to provide better accommodation, better performers with no crude humour allowed, and to introduce ladies evenings, when women – accompanied by a man – could come along and enjoy the shows.

Entry was free, with money made on sale of alcohol and food, and the audience were seated at tables in front of the stage. Gas lighting had taken the place of candles and the stage was also illuminated by gaslight with the early version of spotlights made by a gas flame directed at a cylinder of quick lime (calcium oxide). In later years gas lighting would be replaced by electric but the phrase "stepping into the limelight" continues to this day. Gaslight was extremely dangerous as it was also used at the side of the stage, and the flame occasionally caught the costumes of the actors or the scenery. Many theatres burned down because of the lack of fireproofing.

Entertainers had to project their voices above the din of the crowd, who would talk during performances, and would sing along with the choruses of their favourite tunes, pelting the performers with rotten fruit, manure or (in the emerging industrial towns) rivets, if they didn't like the act. For any entertainer to become successful in their field they had to be able to work extremely hard, have incredible stamina due to the constant travel involved, and a personality to capture the audience's attention – many performers died young from stress and from alcoholism.

Although music hall was becoming more accepted as family entertainment, some things had not changed and the balcony areas were notoriously used by the women of the oldest profession, looking for business.

Harry was still regularly employed by the Royal Christy Minstrels and was gaining valuable experience with them, especially when they were booked in to perform at one of the most famous music halls, the beautiful Alhambra in Leicester Square. He had already seen the same type of decoration in St James' Hall, but now he saw the real thing: it was huge and ornate with two towers and a dome, far larger than the surrounding buildings. It was also, however, one of the more risqué halls, showing scantily clad can-can dancers, which made it extremely popular with men but also controversial and there were many calls for the building to close.

Nathaniel, who had worked so hard to become accepted as middle class, was horrified when Harry said he wanted to be a solo turn on the music hall stage. He had struggled with the thought of his son as part of a minstrel group, but for Harry to perform in music hall was shameful and embarrassing. He had no option, however, but to accept the situation, because Harry – now 19 and an experienced performer – was determined.

Harry knew it was a risk to go solo. He had a good baritone voice, so singing seemed his most obvious choice of career, but he needed an act out of the ordinary – something unique which would make him stand out from all the others and get noticed. But what? He was not conventionally handsome: his face was naturally expressive but he had the prominent nose characteristic of his Jewish ancestry and he was already losing his wavy brown hair. He then remembered how his family laughed when he pulled faces, mimicking other artistes and well-known people of the day. After experimenting with various types of act, he found that this 'elastic face' caused the most hilarity: he had a natural stage presence and was able to portray various characters such as a 'swell', an ape or an old woman, 'pulling mugs' but using minimal costume change. He gradually developed an act which he called Masks and Faces or just 'Face' and started looking for work as a comic vocalist. As with all artistes, he had to pay for all of his make-up, costume, travel, board and lodging out of any bookings he could get, so he found that an act that required little in the way of make-up or costumes kept his costs down.

To have any chance of survival in the industry, or even any limited chance of success, Harry had to be able to immediately attract the audience, competing in a smoky hall with the noisy clatter of glasses and plates, as the patrons loudly talked, ate and drank around tables. He could no longer depend on the troupe, so he had to learn to project his singing voice and his comic recitations. Sometimes he composed his own music, hiring a lyricist to write the words, but more often he simply bought songs.

The atmosphere in many of the smaller halls was suffocating. An overpowering combination of vapour from the gas lighting, the heat of the limelight to illuminate the stage itself and the smell of working-class men, women and children with no deodorant available, made it an unpleasant place to work. The audience had no hesitation in throwing anything they could lay their hands on at an act they didn't like. This meant Harry had to work extremely hard for their attention, together with spending long hours rehearsing comic songs and impersonations – but he loved it. Any laughter or applause he got made the ordeal of travelling to two or three halls a night to perform his act among the many other artistes, worth every exhausting moment.

The earliest record of his solo work was a mention in the *Hampshire Telegraph* on 21 May 1870 stating that he was to appear two days later at the South of England Music Hall in Portsmouth. It was clearly not his debut as it was billed as a 're-appearance' and said that he had also appeared at the Canterbury Music Hall in London. In October, as part of the Crystal Palace Concert Company, he appeared at the Athaeneum Music Hall in Lynn, Norfolk, and then in December at the Kensington Music Hall, which unusually, was seated like a theatre with no tables. In January 1871 he then took the place of chairman, or master-of-ceremonies, there, introducing the acts: he also sang a couple of comic songs, one of which was *Always Washing*. A review at that time in *The Era* commented that he had a "good voice and manner and pleased them (the audience) much".

As much of his work was Kensington-based, he took a room at Queens Court while the rest of the family, who had moved again, were living in Cambridge Street, Westminster.

He started getting bookings further afield and toured up and down the country. Travelling could be arduous and lengthy, involving several changes of train, all operated by different companies, or long trips by horse and carriage in all weathers. There was not much time for leisure because in addition to studying scripts of songs by candlelight or lamp, he needed to rehearse new numbers. Bookings were sometimes only for two or three nights, a week or two if he was lucky, and lodging and food were basic, generally in a boarding house which catered for entertainers. Harry, however, was confident, young, energetic and adventurous, and he thrived – this was what he was born to do.

The nomadic life on the music hall stage could be a lonely occupation and did not give Harry much time to make friends. He went home to see his family when he could and it was while visiting his uncle at St James' Hall that he met Thomas Pedder Hudson, an American minstrel, singer and champion clog dancer. Hudson was to go on to become one of the most famous and wealthy theatrical entrepreneurs in Australia. Striking up a friendship with Tommy, as he was known, Harry discovered they both shared

Thomas Pedder Hudson

a love of travelling, and both were ambitious, wanting to try their acts abroad.

Music hall in Britain was now well established, yet elsewhere it was mostly unknown. The main country apart from America that people associated with amusement or entertainment was the new British colony of Australia. With the Gold Rush 20 years earlier, people had been flocking there to make their fortunes. The country was still sparsely populated and there were only a few cities and towns where theatre and minstrels were popular. Audiences were even known to shower the stages with gold coins. America had also seen a gold rush, too, but there were great distances between cities where travel was difficult. Harry was still keen to go to America but conceded that Australia was a much better prospect. Harry and Tommy started making plans for an adventure to the other side of the world.

When Harry went home and told his parents, his mother was distraught. The quickest way to Australia was by clipper ship: it was a long and dangerous journey, many ships had been lost, and she did not know when – or if – she would see him again. Harry assured her he was not going alone, and she tried to control her fears because he was so enthusiastic. Nathaniel

Acrobat Charles Braham, who used the stage-name Carl Robarts

19

had by now realised that Harry would do as he wanted; he had demonstrated his talent, so all Nathaniel could do was wish him good luck and bid him write as often as he could.

Harry was not the only member of the family to go on the stage: his brother Charles, though he had followed his father's advice and trained to become a law clerk, had also begun touring the halls as an acrobat: a more risky career venture as, by that time – unlike Harry – Charles had a wife and young child to support. He was signed up by a circus agent and adopted the stage name of Carl Robarts. He became well-established as an acrobat and was admired for his physique (he was even asked by the London Hospital to model for them during lectures on the human form).

CHAPTER FOUR
Down Under

Harry was only 20 and Tommy Hudson a couple of years older. The passage fare to Australia of £16 was well beyond what they could afford when the average annual income for a labourer was about £25. They scoured the papers and managed to obtain a berth on board the clipper St Vincent leaving Plymouth on 6 September 1871, paying £3 as fare and working the rest as 'cuddy servants', the lowliest job on board – washing dishes and doing odd jobs. They worked as much as they could to prepare for the voyage, as they needed to buy clothes and other necessities, saving what they could for when they arrived.

Harry and Tommy boarded the train at Waterloo, bound for Plymouth, on a cold wet day, probably staying at one of the many boarding houses before joining the ship. When they saw the St Vincent, she looked massive: she was new, having been built in 1865 by William Pile and Co of Newcastle, and was of a composite construction – made of timber with a steel hull.

The ship had sustained some damage to its rigging during a thunderstorm at Dungeness and was being repaired; they had never seen so many sails. Because of the number of sails, the clippers were the fastest sailing vessels of their day. It was unbelievable that in just over two months they would be in Australia.

Unlike most of the clippers which were built for the tea trade, this was one of the first built for passengers which also held cargo, consisting of cotton, clothing, food, tobacco, spirits, household goods and agricultural equipment, bound for the new colony. They then saw the pigs and cattle being led on which would be used for food during the trip. Taking their luggage, they went below-deck to a small cabin which would be their temporary home, reporting to the Chief Steward Mr Lovejoy, and chatting to other servants and crew who would be their companions for the journey. The sailors withdrew the gangway, loosened the mooring, and Captain

Alex Louttitt and his Chief Officer Mr Barrett set sail that evening. Though Harry and Tommy were probably excited, they may also have watched the harbour recede with moist eyes. There was a strong wind and choppy sea as they set off – there was no going back, and Harry and Tommy did not know if they would ever see England again.

The ship's passengers were the emigrating wealthy and the upper classes; the cabins and saloon accommodation were salubrious. The clipper sat low in the water for speed and did not have stabilisers; as a result many of the passengers spent the first few days in bed suffering from seasickness. Whether Harry was a good sailor or not is not known, but this first trip did not put him off for he was to travel many thousands of miles throughout his life.

The captain and his crew battled the weather through the Bay of Biscay: the pitching and rolling of the ship in the rough seas meant anything not nailed down flew about. The water then started entering the cabins and it was necessary to shut the portholes. In the close confines of the passenger area, and with some of the passengers ill, the atmosphere became oppressive. The ship's surgeon Dr Spicer was kept busy trying to provide any relief he could. For sea-sickness there was very little he could do but urge the sufferers to ride it out.

The weather calmed as the ship neared Madeira. Harry and the other travellers must have felt a great sense of relief. As the passengers recovered they settled into the voyage, walking on deck, reading books, playing chess or cards, and singing round the piano in the saloon. Days were long as the ship was dependent on the wind. Time was made up at the Cape of Good Hope and the Roaring Forties and they did not encounter any other storms. As the journey continued round the tropics, the heat made conditions stifling below deck. For Harry, Tommy, the cooks and stewards in the galley, it was almost unbearable, but it was not long before they felt the other extreme when the ship then encountered colder weather and everyone was glad of the extra clothing they had brought with them.

Preparing the food in the galley kitchen with the movement of the ship, while trying to fend off any queasiness, was difficult. The animals slaughtered on board, and any birds or fish caught, would have been eaten by the cabin passengers. Any leftovers for themselves would have been a luxury – their food was much simpler fare, such as bread, cheese, oats, barley, biscuits, salt meat and preserved foods, accompanied by coffee, beer, lemonade, rum and desalinated water.

At last they saw their first view of Australia – Kangaroo Island, some 20 miles from Adelaide. The mixture of relief, excitement, and apprehension must have been overwhelming. On arrival in Port Adelaide on 25 November, 23 passengers disembarked, among them aristocrats and their children. It is not known whether Harry and Tommy had given any impromptu performances during the voyage – if the passengers had learned that minstrels were aboard, they might well have encouraged them to provide some entertainment.

As they travelled by train or horse and carriage from the port they entered a new and thriving city, but one with a country feel to it. Adelaide was surrounded by parks and was home to only about 27,000 people. The streets were wider than those in London, so the air seemed fresher, though sanitation was much the same as in England and the night-soil men were a familiar sight. There was a lot of discussion in Parliament at the time about how best to improve the sewer system and whether to use earth closets. Only four years earlier, gas lighting had been put in place and a town hall constructed. A new post office was being built, to be opened the following year, and the city was buzzing with the news that a telegraph service was going to start, enabling telegrams to be sent between England and Australia. Already in use between Britain and America, it would revolutionise communication. The only way for Harry to contact his family was by post which was carried on the steamer ships, and he made sure that news of the ship's safe arrival was sent on to England by the next boat. With the telegraph system, if anything should happen to his family he could be notified – and if necessary return – a lot quicker.

It had been 80 days since they left Plymouth on a cold day in early autumn; now they were in Adelaide in the spring warmth. If their act wasn't a success, then Britain was a long, long way away: they must have been nervous.

There were only a couple of days to get familiar with their surroundings before their debut, which had already been advertised in the press, on 28 November at the Theatre Royal, with the well-established Foley Magnet Troupe.

When Harry and Tommy looked out at the audience on that first night their worst fears were realised – there were hardly any people in the theatre. As they started their performance, Tommy's mainly minstrel-orientated act was loudly applauded and encored by the sparse audience, but nobody knew quite what to make of Harry's mimicry act – it was all very new to them. In Britain he had been widely cheered and this lukewarm response would have been a shock to his natural confidence on such an important day in this country far from his home.

They were somewhat relieved when they realised, on reading the local papers, that one of the main reasons for the poor attendance was that a general election was looming and people were attending political rallies all over the city.

Over the next few days more people came to the theatre and warmed to Harry's performance; he had introduced some minstrel material among his usual comicalities, this being more familiar to the audiences. It appeared to work and he was now getting encores.

The first half of the show featured Harry, Tommy, and trapeze acts. The main attractions, though, were the Foleys – brother and sister Kate and John, who danced and performed comedy. The second half of the show was a play and, from 4 December, this was a spectacular performance of 'Mazeppa' or 'The Wild Horse of Tartary' inspired by Lord Byron's poem. The whole troupe, including Harry and Tommy, took part. The plot concerned Mazeppa, a page to King John II Casimir of Poland. Mazeppa falls in love with a countess, who is married to a man 30 years her senior. Mazeppa is caught, brought before the Count, and as punishment is strapped naked to a wild horse which is then let loose. The Foleys used a real horse named Satellite which they trained and the set was fantastically dressed, with one of the actors strapped to the back of the horse which zigzagged up a steep incline rigged on stage.

Audience numbers varied from day to day and although Harry and Tommy were warmly applauded, they were not getting the success they had anticipated. Their last performance at the Theatre Royal was on 11 December. Undaunted, Harry, Tommy and Chas

E Howson – another entertainer who they had met – decided they would tour the northern country districts over the Christmas season, and then make their way to the larger city of Sydney, hoping they would attract bigger audiences who might be more used to their style of performing. They elected Harry as their manager.

The three men travelled to the many Gold Rush shanty-towns to perform in front of very rough-and-ready crowds, mainly men, still searching for their fortune in the goldfields. Most of the halls were wooden and primitive, built in a hurry to satisfy the needs of the thousands who had flocked there from all over the world, though some of the better halls were more reminiscent of those in England ten years previously.

Harry and Tommy had only been in Australia two months when, after some mixed fortunes – including Chas deciding to split from the group – it was time to go to Sydney. The following year, 1872, was to prove an important one in terms of his profession and his private life, for it was in Sydney that Harry would meet the woman who would become his wife – and who would transform his stage act.

CHAPTER FIVE
When Harry Met Lizzie

Harry and Tommy arrived in Sydney in mid-January. Sydney was the second largest city in Australia after Melbourne, with a population of over 200,000. It was well served for amusements but they found that the theatre-going audience had just lost its main opera house, The Prince of Wales in King Street, which had been destroyed by a fire earlier that month, killing two people. The only theatre left for the upper classes to see opera and ballet was The Victoria Theatre, which was dirty and badly in need of re-decoration. Of the alternatives, there was The Temperance Hall and the Masonic Hall which held concerts, and the small Scandinavian Music Hall and the Café Chantant, which catered for the working classes and gold-miners. Spencer's Waxworks was popular with children, especially as it also showed newly invented gadgets such as mechanical birds and toys and glass-blowing. The Exhibition Building in Prince Albert Park held large events such as galas and bands. The only large building used for general entertainment, but which also housed a library and was used for meetings, was the School of Arts in Pitt Street.

Queens Theatre aka Café Chantant and Theatre Royal, Sydney

Harry and Tommy made their debut at the Café Chantant on 3 February. Built at the back of the old Adelphi Hotel in York Street, between King Street and Market Street, it was previously known as the Royal Adelphi Theatre, with a capacity of 1,900 people. It had a pit, stalls, tiered boxes, upper circle and promenade. There were even backstage facilities and a green room. Its entertainment, though, was music hall and minstrelsy rather than opera and theatre. Now named after the popular French Café Chantant on the Champs Elysées in Paris, it had been newly decorated just four months previously.

In music hall tradition it now offered free admission with a refreshment ticket costing sixpence; patrons were expected to be smartly dressed and – unusually – no alcohol was sold, only tea, coffee and pastries. Alcohol, though, was sold illegally and the audiences could be raucous.

The newspapers had advertised Harry and Tommy's acts and the hall was packed with a cross-section of people from all social classes who came to see them, curious about the entertainment on offer and enticed by the new venue. They stared in wonder as Tommy climbed on a five-foot pedestal and danced amazing routines in wooden clogs, the rest of his body motionless. Harry's facial expressions and songs made the crowd roar with laughter. This time the audiences loved them and clamoured for more; they were encored time and time again.

As their popularity grew, hundreds of people crammed into the hall and many still were turned away each night trying to see their sell-out shows. Some of Harry's songs were about current affairs of the day, such as *Tambaroora Gold* about the Gold mining town of Tambaroora near Hill End:

> It's just about one year ago
> As near as I can guess
> Since I last trod old Sydney Streets
> In sorrow and distress
> I'd squandered all my wealth away
> Misfortune had controlled
> But still a voice sang in my ear
> Bright Tambaroora Gold.

Another, about Brigham Young, leader of the Mormons and founder of Salt Lake City, was so in demand that the song-sheets immediately sold out; this may, of course, have been because of his recent imprisonment for "lascivious cohabitation" – scandalously living with a woman without marrying – which had been reported in the newspapers from America. There was increasing hostility to the Mormon philosophy of polygamy, which Young in particular advocated. He had also been accused of being an accessory to a murder in 1857. The lyrics of the song are unknown but had probably titillated the public imagination.

Harry also sang more obscure songs to showcase his comic versatility such as *Chillingowallabadorie*, *Piccadilly* and *Carrotty Hair*.

The School of Arts was grander than the Café Chantant and Harry and Tommy were booked to appear there on 9 March, accompanying the American Excelsior Minstrels: again they were a great success.

School of Arts, Sydney

Easter was considered a major festival and holiday, with most people taking to the coastal towns for some relaxation. Harry and Tommy were among the entertainers hired to perform at Clontarf on Easter Monday, 1 April. Clontarf itself, named after a town near

Dublin in Ireland, was a large private parkland area near the sea and favourite spot for picnics. Four years previously the area had become known for an horrific assassination attempt which sent shockwaves through the community. There had been jubilant scenes and celebrations when the 23-year-old Prince Alfred, Queen Victoria's second son, had come on the first Royal visit to tour the Colony in October 1867, but on 12 March 1868, while at the park on a charity fundraiser for the sailors' home, he was nearly killed when Irishman Henry James O'Farrell shot him in the back. By sheer luck the bullet deflected off the Prince's braces, avoiding major organs while causing a minor but painful injury to his ribs where the bullet hit him. The fact that His Royal Highness survived made no difference to the justice system: O'Farrell was put on trial and hanged the following month. The Prince, on his departure from Australia a short time later, requested the pistol — and the bullet which had been removed from his body — as a memento of his visit.

Since the attack, the owners had struggled to re-build Clontarf's reputation as a safe place for families: there were still occasional problems with Irish sympathisers but, with more strict controls, it was now regularly enjoyed again.

The day of the show dawned dry, warm and sunny, and with many trees to use for shade it was very pleasant for a day out: such were the crowds that it took three steamers to carry them the nine miles from Sydney to enjoy the amusements. Brass bands played with dancing in the pavilion, there were swings, running and walking games, and high-wire and trapeze acts. Harry sang his most popular songs including *Tambaroora Gold*, *Brigham Young*, *Happy Go Bill* and *Good Evening*, with Tommy's pedestal act also going down well.

Afterwards Harry and Tommy returned to the School of Arts. They finished there on 6 April, travelling with the American Excelsior Minstrels to the gold-rush town of West Maitland, 103 miles from Sydney. They appeared at the Olympic Theatre there until 24 April.

As music hall gained popularity in Australia, a growing band of artistes were coming out to Australia. A music hall company from London, Enderby Jackson's Star Combination Company, had been getting a lot of press coverage, with reports full of praise for its headline star Lizzie Watson.

The Company also included Harry Rickards, his wife Carrie, and Richard Ramsden. They had been appearing at the Theatre Royal in Melbourne which had burnt down and were booked for the School Of Arts in Sydney on 1 June. Harry was not performing there at the time, but a theatre critic – who preferred the more accepted music of opera – wrote a disparaging article about this new form of entertainment, and about the Star Combination Company in particular. The article appeared in the *Australian Town and Country Journal* on 8 June:

> "How do you like **him**" was the general, and eager, and excited query of one's friends on meeting at the doors, between the parts, as though the fate of the nation hung in the scale, dependent on the answer. And the question referred, of course, to Mr. Harry Rickards, the position of the others in the troupe being considered but quite secondary. Mr Ramsden we all know: he was in the chorus of Lyster's Opera Company, and used to take small solo parts occasionally: he does the sentimental business; his voice (which has changed, I think, from something of a tenor), not very powerful, or very sweet. The other three are, to my mind, very much alike in their performances; there is in each plenty of voice of a kind fitted for the due representation of the pieces and characters they represent (songs or music they can scarcely be called,) – loud and noisy, harsh, and sometimes necessarily discordant for effect, a little of it going a great way; their dresses are in the very first style of elegance, and set them off to the greatest advantage; the ladies, too, know how to use those dangerous weapons, the eyes, very skilfully. I think Miss Lizzie Watson the best? She is more natural and less loud, than the others with more real humour and less forced gaiety; amongst her other pieces, was a military song, with a roll of the drum that must have excited the envy of any drummer- boy that heard her; also an imitation Chinese song, that was a little funny. Miss Carrie Rickards appears only in duelogue performances

with her brother (sic); on the latter falls the lions' share of the entertainment. There was here with the last minstrel company a few weeks ago a Mr. Braham who sang or recited very much the same kind of songs as Mr. Rickards, and I have heard some ignorant saucy varlets say that but for the clothes, he sang or shouted his pieces quite as well. Monstrous idea! I, not being skilled in the school, don't venture to express an opinion on this point; I have no doubt I shall hear the party again, and be better able to appreciate the difficulties, and discuss the fine points of the execution as well as the style of the pieces. At all events, it is just the very thing to please the Sydney public, from the highest to the lowest, who having got out of the stupid taste for good music steadily refuse to patronize artistes who rely on its powers for their support, but who will eagerly rush to entertainments like these, which appeal so directly to their sympathies, and in which, we are told by enthusiastic admirers, everyone will find his own particular class reflected. After this it is superfluous to say that a seat in the hall is obtained each evening only with damage to one's hat and after many other personal and serious difficulties and sufferings.

At 32 Lizzie was 10 years older than Harry: many articles describe her as attractive, vivacious

Lizzie Watson in 1873

and funny, and as a beautiful singer and dancer with a good figure. They met soon after she arrived in Sydney and Lizzie was obviously impressed: within a few weeks she had decided to leave the Jackson troupe to form her own with him and her handsome singing boyfriend tenor/baritone Richard Ramsden (c1834-1894).

Her real name was Eliza Stephenson, and like Harry she had come to Australia the previous year. Born in Ireland in 1840, she had been working the halls from childhood after escaping from Ireland to the USA during the potato famine. She then moved to England and in May 1859 married an artillery officer named Henry Hemingway. She had been a popular singer in the UK halls from 1859 but, like Harry, saw her future elsewhere. Now a widow, she was given a chance after meeting up with Harry Rickards, whom she had first met in 1865 at Holborn's Raglan Music Hall.

Rickards (1843-1911) was a famous singer in the UK who had tried to go into theatre management, but had been bankrupted by a disastrous venture. He was later to go on to become the most famous theatre impresario in Australia – best known for hiring Marie Lloyd and Dan Leno and for making a star of Florrie Forde. While appearing at the Alhambra in Hull, he met an Australian who said that a variety troupe in Australia would make him a fortune. With nothing to keep him in the UK, he decided to put together a group and asked Lizzie to come along because he thought her extremely talented. Lizzie would not go without Richard Ramsden who was not someone that Rickards knew, but such was his anxiety for Lizzie to be part of his troupe that he agreed to her terms. Carrie Tudor, Rickard's wife, also joined along with Enderby Jackson to act as manager.

Together they raised enough money to travel in the ironclad tea clipper *Lammermuir*. The ship left London for Melbourne on 6 September. A new town hall had recently been built there, the foundation stone having been laid by Prince Alfred during his near-fatal visit to the colony, and a massive organ had been built by the most famous organ-makers of the day, William Hill and Son of London, for assembly and installation there. The 4,000 pipes and all the other pieces were packed in crates to be taken on the ship. Hill was known for the superior quality of its instruments and for building the organs in Sydney Cathedral, and York Minster in England. The total amount involved, including the nine months to build it, was over £7,000.

As the ship was mainly built for cargo there was not much room, and it was a very uncomfortable and subsequently frightening journey. Just a few days into the six-week trip their captain, James Watt, fell ill. His deputy tried to keep the crew in order, but it was a hopeless task. Some of the crew saw it as a golden opportunity, for there was a whole cargo of rum on board. They broke into it, and it didn't take long before they were drunk. Fights broke out, terrorising the passengers, who tried to hide where they could. For the rest of the crew, trying to get the sails rigged and doing general maintenance was almost impossible. While the drunken men fought their way through the hold, others tried to restrain them; finally they were overcome and dragged to the prison deck. Three of the main troublemakers were clapped in irons for the rest of the voyage. A semblance of normality returned but without any formal leadership, and they were all frightened for their own safety until the ship finally docked in Melbourne on 28 November.

The relief on disembarking was immense and the heat hit the troupe like a sledgehammer. Exhausted, they were met by James Allison a theatrical agent from Adelaide and went to their lodgings at the Old White Hart Hotel in Bourke Street. The following day, Allison introduced them to Mr L M Bayless, lessee and manager of the Princess Theatre, who invited them to appear there at a benefit for his wife. The harrowing journey from England seemed to have been worth it when they debuted on 2 December and were an instant success. Before long, Lizzie was headlining, Richard Ramsden was applauded, Rickards re-established his reputation as a comic singer, and he and Jackson became well-known managers. Lizzie, Ramsden and the Rickards company were appearing at the School of Arts while Harry and Tommy were at the Café Chantant.

By the time June came around, Lizzie was determined to leave the company, though she was under contract to Rickards and Jackson and had become their star attraction. After a raging argument, she did her last show and then left acrimoniously, taking Richard Ramsden with her.

Harry in Masonic regalia

Harry had decided to follow in his father's footsteps and join the Freemasons, though he had to wait until after his 21st birthday when came of age. There was one main lodge in Sydney – The Lodge of Harmony no 556. He asked to join, and was initiated on 4 July 1872.

For the first time, on 17 July, Lizzie, Harry, Tommy and Richard Ramsden were all on the same bill at the Masonic Hall for a Complimentary Benefit being performed for John Barnett, a well-known baritone. In the audience was the elite of Sydney society including the Mayor, Sir Hercules and Lady Robinson and the Hon Henry Parkes, the Colonial Secretary, who was to be the future five-times Prime Minister and 'Father of the Federation of Australia'.

When it came time for Lizzie's act, she was nowhere to be seen. The audience was getting impatient when, after some time, John Barnett came to the front of the stage and stated that Lizzie was unable to perform through indisposition. He then had to persuade a number of singers who were not on the programme to appear; a band was also asked to perform a few numbers.

Harry on stage, around 1872

The considerable delay caused the audience of 400 to become extremely irritable and there was some slow-handclapping and jeering. They were only appeased when Harry appeared on stage to sing *Good Evening*, for which he was encored, giving them a humorous character song called *Sarah Walker*, which cheered the audience immensely. Tommy then appeared with his pedestal dance and was also encored. It is unknown whether Lizzie was truly ill or if she had had another disagreement with someone: this had happened previously in the UK.

A few days later Lizzie was appearing in her own act at the Royal Victoria Theatre, while Harry and Tommy were at the Theatre Royal. She began forming her company and signed up Harry, Richard Ramsden, her singing pupil Lizzie Dixon, and another singer, Lydia Howarde. Tommy did not join them, returning to the Theatre Royal to perform in his own act there.

Lizzie's new company boarded the steamer *Maitland* bound for Newcastle, 101 miles from Sydney, on 16 August for their debut that same evening at the town's own School of Arts, but their tour got off to a bad start when Ramsden fell down the stairs from his cabin when the boat lurched: he was seriously injured, cutting his head and face. The injury meant he was unable to appear and he only recovered sufficiently to perform when the troupe travelled to West Maitland for a performance ten days later before returning to Newcastle for their last appearance, which included – as well as their comic songs – a 'Scotch Comedy – The Bonnie Fish Wife' in which Harry played a character called Sir Hiccory Heartycheer.

The *Newcastle Chronicle* on 20 August said of Harry that he "was in excellent voice and gave his comic songs with much spirit. He was as much at home in the song 'Old Sarah Walker' as he was in the distinguished Swell located in Piccadilly".

By the time they returned to Sydney. Lizzie had changed her troupe slightly and it now consisted only of Lizzie Dixon, Harry and Harry Ackland, a tenor. Ramsden did not rejoin the company until 21 September in Bathurst – it may be that he had not fully recovered from his fall.

The Victoria Theatre was showing the opera 'Faust' and the critic 'Biron' of the *Australian Town and Country Journal* who had, in a previous article, commented less than favourably on Rickards' troupe, now stated in his column on 7 September: "Nothing daunted by having to face so formidable an opposition as a grand opera in the immediate neighbourhood, Miss Lizzie Watson, full of the

British spirit which is not easily crushed, appeals to her friends and supporters, offering them a week's entertainment at The School of Arts with her newly organized company including now a favourite Sydney tenor, Mr Ackland. Miss Dixon is said to be already much improved, and Mr Braham to appear quite a new man under present auspices; so that a pleasant evening is ensured to those who are admirers of a miscellaneous entertainment of this character. Miss Watson certainly deserves success".

Was Harry seeming to be 'quite a new man' a sign that there was more than a friendship between him and Lizzie? Maybe with Ramsden out of action they had become closer? Ramsden was not just her business partner but had been her boyfriend since before they had left England: Harry was 10 years younger than him and a stronger singer and performer – it may also have been that Harry was smitten by Lizzie's obvious charms.

Biron then reported of Lizzie the following week that "her grace and piquante manner (despite some peculiarities in her pronunciation) will always make her a favourite everywhere; and, neither in the manner of her songs, or in the manner of her singing them, is there one tittle of vulgarity, or departure from good taste, the same may be said of her dressing, which is elegant and tasteful, and quite comme il faut, as a lady and not in fancy character," and of Harry that "Mr. Harry Braham's very funny character-songs and Mr. Ackland's sentimental ballads aid in making an excellent entertainment".

As this particular critic was known to be biased towards opera, and many people still considered music hall to be common, regarding the performers as low-class and some of the women little better than prostitutes, this was high praise indeed.

Even though life was hectic with continuous travelling, rehearsing and performing, Harry was still studying Freemasonry and he was admitted to the highest level he could aspire to, the third degree, on 18 September 1872 in the Lodge of Harmony. The most famous man to be initiated into the same Lodge was the first Prime Minister of Australia, Sir Edmund Barton, just six years later, in 1878.

The troupe – Lizzie, Harry, Lizzie Dixon, and Ramsden – along with Tommy who had now joined them – left Sydney for an engagement at Lewis' Pavilion in Bathurst, 126 miles from Sydney. Fortunately there was now a direct link by carriage because Cobb & Co, the famous carriage-makers, had taken advantage of the miners' need to transport gold to the banks, and had based their business in the town. The journey, changing horses every 10 miles at the various staging-posts on dirt tracks over hilly terrain, was long, tiring, dusty and uncomfortable, with the ever-present danger of bushrangers – highwaymen or runaway convicts, of whom Ned Kelly was the most famous. At least they could all travel together because up to 20 people could travel in a single carriage. The company, because of the number of horses they had, were well known for their punctuality, even if journeys tended to begin as early as 5am.

Bathurst was the first major gold-mining town: it was the gold found there in the 1850s that had started the gold-rush, causing massive expansion of the town which now boasted over half a mile of shops. Bathurst had more hotels than any other outside the main cities, though its largest building was the prison. Miners during the early gold-rush years in the outlying camps away from the cities could become homesick and depressed; sometimes they worked for little gain and they could be volatile as they sweated in the goldfields. Crime soared in direct relation to how much gold was being mined and a number of men were killed in fights in the surrounding areas, the murderers eventually finding themselves in Bathurst prison. Executions were commonplace. It was hardly an atmosphere for women or children, but when the miners started to bring their families out, it brought more stability, though life was still rough. The hardworking miners and their families badly needed entertainment as well, and eagerly awaited the troupe's arrival. They did not disappoint, even reducing the prices of tickets in the gallery from three shillings to one shilling on the last night of their show, to give as many people as possible the chance to see them.

Harry and Tommy were still appearing on stage by themselves when they could, but Tommy's ambitions to become a manager meant that they decided to part.

Returning to Sydney, Harry stayed in the city, fulfilling engagements from 14 October at the newly named Theatre Royal (previously Café Chantant). Meanwhile Lizzie had other plans for herself.

The local press rumoured that she was going try and patch things up with Rickards and had made arrangements to re-join his troupe, though in reality Rickards had gone to Auckland; instead she left Sydney on 10 October for Melbourne with Ramsden, accompanied by a servant. The truth was that Lizzie wanted to prove herself in the 'legitimate theatre'. She was engaged to appear at The Princess's Opera House playing Josephine in the operetta 'Daughter of The Regiment'. She had already appeared in the same operetta in Sydney and it had been a popular success, although it was not critically acclaimed. The press reported that her acting was "self-possessed" and that she could not "play" the part, being more at home on the music-hall stage, for which her style of singing was more appropriate. Her performance was called "vulgar and loud with uncouth gestures", with her pronunciation of some words harsh to the ear. This was probably due to her Irish accent pronouncing 'regiment' as 'ridgiment'. Her act on the music-hall stage was judged just the opposite, with her singing called sweet and her manners graceful. Clearly, though the two forms of entertainment crossed paths, there was still a class barrier.

When the operetta finished its run, Lizzie felt she had finished with legitimate theatre and was clearly more comfortable when the programme changed to the more familiar music-hall acts and burlesque of 'Aladdin'.

On 7 January 1873, Lizzie and Harry sailed for Brisbane with a small company including her servant, Ramsden, and two young Japanese children - Yamo Moto who performed tricks, and Kami Sami, a tightrope walker – who had both been starring with Harry. They made their debut at the School of Arts later that month. Lizzie's repertoire included a variety of songs in which she danced the hornpipe in Roman costume and then played the side-drum: the most requested of these was *KCB*:

> *My love he was a Farmer*
> *But now he's gone away*
> *For one and a penny a day*
> *He's tired of agricultural life*

And says that he'll obtain
The highest honour to be had
Ere he returns again.

Chorus
He's gone to join the army
And a soldier he will be
A corporal, a Sergeant
Or an ADC
A Captain or a Colonel
Or something else you see
He'll never rest till he becomes
A KCB.

He's thrown aside the hoe and rake
Likewise the spade and plough
To all such occupations
He never means to bow
His soul's so full of ardour
All danger he does scorn
And now he sighs for fields of war
Instead of fields of corn

I told him he was foolish
To go and leave the farm
For I should break my heart
If e'er he came to harm
But still he is devoted
In love to me you see
And when he is promoted
Then he will marry me.

On 29 January Harry announced that he was to have a complimentary benefit and Lizzie announced that the evening of 5 February was set apart for her own. They also said that this would be their final show at the theatre. The reason behind the benefits became clear the following day: less than nine months after they met, Harry and Lizzie were married by special licence in Brisbane Register office.

They chose the popular seaside town of Sandgate, 15 miles from Brisbane, for their honeymoon.

Was Lizzie's parting from Ramsden amicable? Maybe he had even been at the wedding, though as he returned to Sydney and never appeared with them again, he may have found Lizzie and Harry's marriage was too much to bear.

CHAPTER SIX
A Venture into Burlesque

On 18 February 1873, Harry and Lizzie made the 300-mile journey by boat from Brisbane to the towns of Maryborough, Gladstone and Rockhampton, accompanied by two popular young dancing sisters, Rachel and Heloise. There is no record of how these performances were received, but on their return to Brisbane to open at the Victoria Hall on 24 March (when they were joined by Henry Chapman, a conjuror), the audience reaction was so enthusiastic that it prompted one reporter in the *Brisbane Courier* on 28 March to describe the Brahams thus:

> Mr Harry Braham gave evidence of his great versatility of talent as an actor, as well as a singer, in the course of the evening. He changes, not only his appearance, but his voice so well, that it is difficult to tell that the same performer is the swell "At the Ball", the gruff "General Jinks," and the querulous old lady of the name of "Sarah Walker".

Such was their reception and popularity that, though they had to finish at the Victoria Theatre on 5 April, they transferred to the School of Arts for another six performances, with Harry named as proprietor of the company. The climax of the variety performance was a comic ballet called 'Love in a Tub' with Harry performing two parts – Miss Duelittle (a coquette) and Simkin (a Jack o' wires). Rachel and Heloise performed the part of Jack (a sailor) and Hebri-Bright (a Quaker), while J Tolano – who was also the company's agent – played Mr Duelittle (a farmer). Harry and Lizzie's songs, solos as well as duets, were becoming so popular that even the 'larrikins' (hoodlums) were heard singing them in the streets. *The Brisbane Courier* reported on 16 April:

> Harry Braham and his wife (late Miss Lizzie Watson) seem to grow more popular the longer they remain here, and their little company at The School of Arts attracts as

large and more enthusiastic audiences than ever. Nobody before has succeeded so well in hitting the popular taste of Brisbane playgoers and retaining so firm a hold on their attention. This is partly due, no doubt, to the character of the entertainment given. Music halls have not taken root here yet, and this is the first time we have had a really good specimen of this class of performances. Hundreds of persons who would not care to sit out a play, however carefully and well rendered, will go night after night to hear a few good comic songs well sung, and witness some clever dancing. But the chief cause of Mr. and Mrs. Braham is unquestionably the ability and good taste which characterizes all they undertake. Their repertory of songs seems absolutely inexhaustible, Harry himself, is an admirable mimic, and Mrs Braham, in addition to a very attractive face and figure great vivacity and never failing good humour is equally happy in broadly comic, serio-comic or patriotic songs and the two are good at comic duets.

The public did not notice that there were tensions within the group. The two sisters, Rachel and Heloise, rowed constantly. This caused difficulties for Harry and Lizzie, and when the sisters broke their engagement, they were sacked from the company. The company put an advertisement in the *Brisbane Courier* on 21 April 1873 to this effect: "Mr. and Mrs. Harry Braham beg to state that Miss Rachel and Miss Heloise, having broken their engagement are no longer connected with them in their concerts."

After this stress so soon after their marriage, Harry and Lizzie decided to abandon the idea of managing a troupe – instead, they would tour by themselves.

Taking the steamer *City of Brisbane* to Sydney, Harry and Lizzie began engagements at the School of Arts with 'Thiodons Wonders' a popular puppet theatre including the Crystal Palace Giants from London, Gog and Magog – who took their names from the traditional mythical guardians of the city – and the Highland Dwarfs in duets and dances On the last day, 3 May, the show's proprietor Aspinall Thiodon put on a special matinee for children.

After a short break, they then travelled to Hill End, near Bathurst, to appear possibly in the Great Varieties Hall, its name belying the reality of a theatre set up in a canvas tent. If Lizzie and Harry had known what the town was like, they may have thought twice about making the long journey from the comparative luxury of Sydney. Hill End's buildings were ramshackle, built of poor timber with bark or corrugated iron roofs; the one main street usually flooded and got choked with mud because the area was notorious for its heavy rain. The town, though, had become famous six months previously when German miner Bernhardt Holtermann found a huge gold nugget, henceforth known as the Holtermann Nugget. At 59 inches long and weighing 630 pounds with approximately 5,000 ounces of gold content, it was the largest gold specimen ever discovered. As a consequence, Hill End had enlarged to such an extent that there were 51 registered hotels, five banks, 28 pubs, an oyster bar and an opium den. Perhaps its prosperity influenced their decision, or perhaps they just enjoyed the adventure of singing in a crowded town that was still excited by the gold discovery.

From Hill End, they moved to Bathurst, but many people were disappointed when the extremely wet weather that week meant horses could not get through the mud and forced them to cancel one of the shows.

By now they were being paid nearly £50 a week, and were being booked to boost audiences if another artiste failed to bring in enough money. They still had to pay their own expenses, but were now able to afford better accommodation in the various hotels and lodging houses.

Generally known by her stage name, Lizzie Watson, she added a codicil and was now known as 'Lizzie Braham (Late Lizzie Watson)'. She was better-known than her husband, so she usually topped the bill. Harry changed his comedy routines every night and the show always included a duet.

The *Sydney Morning Herald* reported on 13 June that their engagement had been secured at the Theatre Royal in York St for 24 nights at a cost to the management of £200 – the equivalent of a government official's yearly wage. On the opening night the doors had to be closed early after there was no more room, standing

Harry in drag in Pygmalion and his Gal(adear!) in 1873

or sitting, and carriages were blocking the street. Nearing the end of the run they had become so popular that the management — at further cost — were forced to extend their performances.

Harry and Lizzie had already enjoyed playing comedy roles apart from their usual songs and decided to stage their first burlesque — a parody of a serious play or a work of classical literature — on 1 August 1873.

'Pygmalion and his Galatear' was a romantic satire in which a statue (Galatear) comes to life and disrupts the life of its sculptor Pygmalion when his wife Cynisca is away. When Cynisca returns she is extremely jealous of Galatear, who — less than 24 hours later — decides her previous state was better, and turns back into a statue. The play, based on Greek mythology was a huge success for its author W S Gilbert (of Gilbert and Sullivan fame), who produced it in 1871 — it was estimated to have earned him £40,000 during his lifetime. The Australian writer Garnet Walch adapted the play as a pantomime burlesque especially for Harry Rickards, renaming it Pygmalion and his Gal(adear!) with the male part (Galatear) played in drag. It was first put on at the New Apollo Hall in Melbourne on 31 March 1873 by Rickards and his company, to initial success, but it failed when it transferred to Adelaide and Rickards decided not to perform it again. Harry and Lizzie were keen to perform it, however, and Rickards, who held the copyright, either sold or gave them the play — whether this was in friendship is not known, because of the row the previous year. With Harry as Galadear and Lizzie as Pygmalion it was so successful that the five-night run was extended until 24 August. Walch used some music by Offenbach in the play and Harry sang this to the tune of 'The Magic Melody' or 'Fortunio's Song'.

> *I am a statue come to life*
> *To be this sculptor's little wife*
> *I'm made already*
> *A maiden steady,*
> *In this queer world of noughts and crosses,*
> *I've come to learn my lesson pat*
> *That little fellow there, my boss is*

Just ask him what he thinks of that
I'll learn my letters, I'll ape my betters
I'll make Pygmalion such a wife
I am a statue come to life
I am a statue come to life
Fal la,la,la,la,la,la,la foi di riddle lol di – statue come to life.

After this excursion into the burlesque, Harry and Lizzie returned to music-hall fayre.

Their popularity showed no sign of diminishing and the building was crowded nightly; because of this the management did not end their contract and salary was now no object. One of Harry's most requested songs was 'Parisian 'Arry', also known as 'The Cockney Abroad' written by prolific composter G W Hunt.

The *Sydney Morning Herald* of 26 September said: "Glorious Glorious success of Mr and Mrs Braham's new medley duet, pronounced by all who have heard it to be the very achme (sic) of vivacious acting, ridiculous gestures, and sweet vocalization."

On 10 November they appeared, with other artistes, at the magnificent galleried exhibition hall in Prince Alfred Park before over 4,000 people. Harry and Lizzie were among the first acts on, under a platform at the western side of the gallery, and were warmly applauded by those who were able to hear them, the hall being so big. Acrobats Madame Zulu and George Loyal performed feats on the trapeze high above the audience. When Madame Zulu appeared to lose her footing, shouts of alarm could be heard in the galleries before audible sighs of relief when she regained her balance. Later, a German band took to the centre of the room which was turned into a dance area; amorous couples danced on the floor and in the galleries, providing a colourful spectacle. In one of the private rooms in the hall a "bonnie baby" contest was even held. The music and dancing went on until after 10.30pm, when there were still over 2,000 people in the hall – perhaps Harry and Lizzie took some time out after their act to join the couples enjoying themselves.

After nearly seven months in Sydney, Harry and Lizzie were still getting good audiences but needed a fresh challenge. They had met a few other artistes during their run in the Theatre Royal who they got on well with and they were keen to try managing a group again. It was important, though, to go somewhere different. New Zealand was becoming an increasingly popular destination, and Harry Rickards had already had some success there. It seemed an ideal opportunity. They named their ensemble The Queen's Variety Troupe and invited Alex O'Brien (also known as Alick, a contortionist), Mme Blanche (occasionally known as Mlle, a trapeze artist), Mat Riley (an Irish comic singer), Mons Hamew (an acrobat known as the Flying Beadle), and Charles T Baker, (a Negro 'delineator' or impersonator) to appear with them.

The troupe stayed at the Occidental Hotel in Sydney before sailing on the steamship *Wentworth* to their first booking at the Prince of Wales Theatre, Auckland, on 4 December 1873. The town was still recovering after a major fire in Queen Street had destroyed 58 buildings, including three hotels, just three months earlier.

The review in the *Auckland Star* the day after the first show stated that the cheering was "so loud and prolonged has seldom, if ever, been heard within the walls of a theatre the enthusiasm which everywhere prevailed being evidenced in the waving of handkerchiefs and the clapping of hands and the excited shouts of WELCOME MISS WATSON & MR BRAHAM!" Lizzie was greeted with an ovation on entering.

The same paper on 11 December said that Harry "produces something new nightly, and never fails to elicit roars of genuine and approving applause".

The troupe then decided to put the burlesque 'Pygmalion' back on for Christmas, reviving it to immense success before travelling to do shows in Wellington and then in Christchurch. Having completed their tour of the north, it was time to travel south to the furthest city in the world from London, and the largest in New Zealand – Dunedin – to appear at the Princess Theatre from 8 -16 February 1874. It was during this tour that Lizzie had another argument – this time with a conductor – and it was left to Harry to calm things down before the performance could go ahead. They then went to the Queens Theatre on 18 February before travelling back to Australia.

After only two months as managers and despite their success, as soon as they returned to Australia they disbanded the troupe and on 18 March opened at St George's Hall, Melbourne, by themselves to further critical acclaim. Tommy briefly joined them for a couple of dates in April at St George's Hall in Benalla, when they advertised themselves as the 'Star Comique Entertainment'. From Benalla they transferred to the Apollo in Melbourne and a review in the *Melbourne Argus* said: "The bright particular star is Mr Harry Braham whose exuberance in manner and action leads him to the very extreme of broad farce. Besides this he has the most extraordinary talent for facial contortion being able to transform his countenance into shapes most grotesque. The audience which quite filled the room seemed to appreciate his eccentricities as indeed they did almost everything that came before them for nearly all the songs and dances were encored".

After their triumphs in Australia and New Zealand, they were ambitious to try somewhere else. Harry told Lizzie it had always been his dream to go to the USA. The famous Billy Emerson Minstrels were also appearing at the Apollo and in June were due to go to San Francisco aboard the steamship *Tartar* via Honolulu.

Harry and Lizzie asked Billy if they could accompany them, and he agreed.

Could they conquer the USA?

CHAPTER SEVEN
Aloha Harry

Harry and Lizzie's voyage to San Francisco and their hope for further acclaim nearly came to an early end when at 3am on 22 June they were jolted awake in their cabin. The ship had struck something and the engines suddenly stopped. Nobody seemed to be panicking, so they dressed as quickly as they could and made their way to the saloon, where they found all the other passengers looking anxiously at Captain Ferries wondering what had happened and where they were. He told them that they had collided with a coral reef and were about a hundred miles from the nearest island. Shocked and scared, they listened carefully and were a little relieved when he told them tests had shown the ship to be watertight, but that they would need to get free from the reef.

The Captain tried to dislodge the ship by reversing the engines – but it was stuck fast. After taking a lifeboat at daylight around the ship to survey their position, he decided the only way they could continue their journey was to lighten the ship. At around 6am all the male passengers offered to help, forming themselves into groups: Harry found himself shovelling coal into baskets to discharge into the sea. They were already tired and it was back-breaking, exhausting, dirty work in the heat, but with Lizzie and the other women passengers encouraging them and bringing food and drink of oatmeal water, tea and coffee, they pressed on. By 10am the following day the ship was 400 tons lighter. Two boats were sent out to survey the sea for a clear way through. One of them was smashed when a high roller hit it: the boat was wrecked but the man on board was rescued.

When the tide came in, the stokers put the steam engines into full gear and the ship – which had never ceased bumping – rocked as the current forced her forward. The passengers watched and listened with bated breath as she ground over the reef, sending coral everywhere. There was a heart-stopping moment when the machinery failed, but then miraculously she floated. The drama was far from over, however, because she had floated into a lagoon that was surrounded by other reefs. Another launch was put out, which cautiously tried to find a safe passage, but it was now too dark and the Captain anchored until morning. A bell sounded for prayers and Rev John Raven led a moving service while everyone, many still ingrained with coal dust, knelt and prayed. On 24 June, the launch once again put forward, managing – with the aid of empty oil cans – to find a way to open water, but it took nearly three hours and more than one false move before the Captain managed to navigate through. Harry and the other passengers cheered as she finally cleared the reefs and steamed into the ocean.

Four days later, the ship docked in Hawaii to be examined, to disembark the passengers who were due to land there, and to take on more supplies. The Captain was asked to explain his actions at a trial and was exonerated when it was deemed that a combination of foggy conditions and an uncharted reef had caused the collision. He and the crew were praised for getting the ship and its passengers to safety with no damage. There was severe criticism about lack of lifeboats for the number of passengers on board, but nevertheless the ship left for San Francisco the following day.

Harry, Lizzie and the Billy Emerson Minstrels were due to continue to San Francisco, but did not reboard the ship, probably wanting time to recover from their exhausting and anxious voyage, and they checked in at the Hawaiian Hotel. They were not booked to perform in Hawaii, but nevertheless appeared at the Royal Hawaiian Theatre on 7 July.

The islands had just gone through a traumatic period of adjustment, reigned over by three different kings in two years. King Kamehemaha IV, the last monarch of the dynasty, had died in December 1872 and had not named a successor, so under Hawaiian law another king had to be elected. The two main candidates were high chiefs William C Lunaillo and David Kalakaua: in the 1873 election, Lunaillo won by a landslide, only to die a year later, leaving Kalakaua to succeed him.

The new king was not popular at first, though his people gradually warmed to him when he started visiting their villages and affirming his loyalty to them. His love of song, music and dance, earned him the nickname 'The Merrie Monarch'. He was to bring the ukulele to the islands and to re-introduce the hula, which had been banned by a previous monarch.

Perhaps the king had heard about the group when he commanded a performance? The *Pacific Commercial Advertiser* on 11 July talked of the: "Unbounded Success of Emerson's English Combination Under The Patronage and in the Presence of His Majesty the King & Suite," and said that "By Request of His Majesty The King, Harry Braham will sing *Piccadilly*."

Lizzie sang *Good Bye My Love* and a comic sketch, 'A Trip to Paris', was performed with Billy Emerson playing Major Bill, Mr Williams as the Colonel, Harry as Policeman Beat and Lizzie as Madame Lorraine.

The troupe performed again before the king a week later, with their final show on 21 July before sailing on to San Francisco.

CHAPTER EIGHT
Yankee Doodle Harry

Harry and Lizzie arrived in San Francisco which, like Australia, had benefited from a gold-rush 20 years previously. It was now the premier banking city in the United States, with the San Francisco Mint producing coins from the mass of gold found, and Wells Fargo bank built among many others. In September the first cable car was introduced, and with the new railway under construction, the city buzzed with life.

Now a well-established act, Harry and Lizzie were billed as The Brahams, and found their fame had preceded them. They were booked at the Bella Union Theatre, the most popular theatre for minstrel variety and burlesque in the city. The theatre was in the rough, notorious red-light district of Barbary Coast, between Washington and Kearny Streets. Gambling, opium dens and riotous saloons abounded, its clientele mostly miners and sailors desperate for drunken entertainment and women – sailors in particular had to beware, for shanghaiing was rife in the area.

Although The Brahams' performing style was always said not to be lewd, they had to have a certain amount of cheeky sauciness in their act to appeal to the type of audiences which crowded the theatre. One of Lizzie's songs would no doubt have been popular with the sailors:

> I'm one of those downright jolly girls
> That follow fashion's sway
> Whatever is the thing in vogue
> If it be dull or gay
> Well boating is tip top just now
> So in for it I go
> I'm coxswain of the hero club
> My name is Saucy Flo!

They stayed an unprecedented 47 weeks. When they ended their contract on 11 July 1875 the theatre proprietor, Samuel Tetlow, gave them a glowing report in a large advertisement in the *New York Clipper*, the main theatrical newspaper, lauding their act for future engagements.

Tetlow was to become embroiled in a scandal just five years later when he shot and killed his business partner, Billy Skeantlebury. He was acquitted on the grounds of self-defence, but ended his life in poverty when he fell in love with a chorus girl who led him into financial ruin after his wife's death.

The newspaper advertisement came to the attention of theatrical agents Simmonds and Wall, who were based in Union Square, New York. They took on Harry and Lizzie, who arrived in New York on 20 July, probably going most of the way by the new trans-American railway. This journey a few years previously would have taken months from San Francisco by horse and carriage, or weeks by sea, and now only took a week.

Poster for Harry's 'Silly Bill and Father' act, 1875

They performed for the first time in New York at the Globe Theatre on 28 August. For their debut, Harry came up with an act for himself called 'Silly Bill and Father'. He had a model made which, when attached in front and behind, gave the illusion of a very fat boy riding on the back of a thin old man. His inspiration for this was the Italian theatrical form of comedy Commedia Dell'Arte – in which masks were used to improvise various characters such as Pierrot and Harlequin – and the style of Steele Mackaye's character-acting, that relied on pose and gesture to communicate emotion, which he had seen on stage. Mackaye (1842-1894) was

53

one of the most important actors and playwrights of his generation: he had learned his craft in Paris from François Delsarte and he went on to establish the American Academy of Dramatic Art, teaching this style of acting. Drawing on this method, and using his own talent for mimicry, Harry proceeded to convey his characters through a myriad of expressions and gestures while singing.

Harry and Lizzie's agents were quick to book them on tour, first to the Howard Athaeneum in Boston, and then to the Theatre Comique in St Louis, Montana, before going to Fox's American Theatre in Philadelphia, where Lizzie starred as Prince Ko Ko in the Christmas burlesque of 'Robinson Crusoe'. Her performance was hailed for her fine singing, graceful acting and dancing; Harry's comic songs were encored six or seven times a night.

They returned to New York after five weeks when they were booked to appear at the Broadway theatre of vaudeville legend and impresario Tony Pastor. The theatre was in a prime position opposite the large Metropolitan Hotel in the fashionable 'ladies mile' with many shops and department stores, and was crowded every night. Tony Pastor (1833-1908) was the 'father of vaudeville' and the American equivalent of Charles Morton, in that he only hired the best: to enable women and children to be entertained, he cleaned up vaudeville and allowed no vulgarity. He had started his career in the circus before becoming a comic singer and songwriter, eventually buying his own theatre. Any artistes who were able to say they had worked for Tony could be guaranteed further success, and Harry and Lizzie impressed Tony so much that he asked them to go on his summer tour with him. So after they had been to their next engagements in Buffalo, Chicago and Brooklyn, they met up with Tony and his troupe at the Arch Theatre in Philadelphia.

The troupe continued to Kansas City and Virginia, and other towns and cities before finishing at San Francisco's Bush Street Theatre. Tony, though, had decided that as Harry and Lizzie had appeared there so recently, they should skip this and re-join him later, and their last performance with him was on 18 May at the Griswold Opera House in Troy, New York.

This meant that they missed the wild celebrations in San Francisco when the first trans-continental train crossed the country directly from New York, arriving there in only 83 hours, on 4 June 1876. Harry's father had decided to travel to America to see him, and it was in the midst of a heatwave on 26 June that Harry and Lizzie went to Castle Garden Immigration Centre at the tip of Manhattan Island to await his arrival on the steamship *The City of Berlin*.

As Harry saw the portly figure of Nathaniel come through the gates there would have been emotional scenes as father and son were re-united after five years. Letters were not the same as being able to talk face-to-face: news of the rest of his family may have overwhelmed him and it must have been disappointing that his mother was not there – maybe she had been unable to leave Edwin? At least the early disagreements over Harry's chosen career were now forgotten.

Harry introduced Lizzie to him, then they spent some time showing Nathaniel the city and the surrounding area. Ships were arriving all the time bringing new settlers and building work was everywhere. If they had crossed the river from Manhattan into Brooklyn, they would have seen the massive Brooklyn Bridge still under construction.

Nathaniel had never been outside Great Britain and the sights, money and accents would have all been very strange to him, the papers full of American headlines including the shocking news that the famous General Custer and his whole command had been killed at Little Big Horn by the American Indians just the day before Nathaniel had arrived in New York.

Only a few days later, smoke could be seen billowing from the Castle Garden area and they would have found out that the Immigration Centre where Nathaniel had arrived had burnt to the ground.

Before Nathaniel returned to England he visited Trenton in New Jersey, and as a reminder of his trip he went to a photographer to get a picture taken of himself for Harry.

Harry and Lizzie then went to the National Theatre in Philadelphia on 15 July before re-joining Tony's troupe in September at his theatre, taking time out in November to appear at the Holliday

Street Theatre in Baltimore. Harry continued with his novel 'Silly Bill' act, which had become so successful in its own right that an advertising poster was made.

Lighting of theatres had not changed and gas jets were used at the stage: fires were commonplace. Audiences and performers were always aware of the hazard and it was an accepted risk, though sometimes a fire was so horrifying and tragic it made all the papers. The theatrical world was rocked when the Brooklyn Theatre – said to have had some of the most up-to-date safety features – caught fire on 5 December, killing 250 people. On their return from Baltimore, Harry and Lizzie could not have failed to see the ruins and perhaps knew some of the performers killed on that fatal night. After the fire, audience levels dropped dramatically in the city.

Harry and Lizzie were keen to leave New York, and once again went on tour with Tony, parting from him in San Francisco, where they sailed on alone to Hawaii for a series of engagements again at the Royal Hawaiian Theatre. Nathaniel's visit the previous year may well have made Harry homesick, and they decided to come back to the UK – but first they made one more trip to Sydney, leaving on the SS *Zealandia* on 12 September 1877.

Harry's father Nathaniel and his mother Susan, pictured in 1876

Arriving in Sydney on 11 October, they returned to the Queen's Theatre, which had undergone alterations since its days as the Café Chantant/Theatre Royal. It was now decorated in white, gold and grey, with red plush seating and with a glass chandelier as a centrepiece. On 8 November, Lizzie took a grand farewell benefit. During the evening, various contests were performed, with the prizes being silver tea and coffee services: one contest involved skating, in which the whole stage was used.

Six days later they appeared at the Queen's Theatre for a benefit in aid of the Indian Famine Relief Fund, with songs and a farce called 'The Steeplechase'.

Artistes had many 'farewells, and last evenings', mainly to encourage as big an audience as possible to boost takings, so there followed a further week of 'farewell performances', culminating three days later with a special midday performance for schools and families before the final evening performance. They had already booked to leave on the steamship *Hankow* which was also carrying cargo for the 1878 Paris World's Fair, which would showcase Australian fine arts and new machinery.

On 20 December they left the country for the last time. They were now among the highest-paid performers of their profession, and — having first sailed to Australia in clipper ships — were now able to afford the luxury of saloon accommodation on a steamship, costing over 30 guineas a ticket.

While they were on the ship, a critical newspaper article appeared in *The Era* about their act at the Queen's Theatre, and this damning paragraph angered them: "Lizzie Watson and Harry Braham have been a most signal failure at the Queen's Theatre, Sydney New South Wales, and Mr Bayless, will, doubtless, not be sorry when their season is over. He has some big cards coming, and deserves to succeed, for he spares no expense or trouble to give satisfaction." To set the record straight, this large advertisement was sent in reply, detailing their success in America:

> The Brahams Harry and Lizzie the world renowned
> musical sketch artistes just concluded a four year
> successful tour throughout America having during that

period fulfilled the following unparalleled engagements: Eleven Months' Starring Engagement at the Bella Union San Francisco and just terminated a Return Engagement of Five months at the same theatre; Six Months with Tony Pastor's troupe and have likewise appeared at the Academy of Music, New York, and principal Variety theatres throughout the USA (all Fourth and Fifth Engagements).

The Brahams returned 20th October 1877 to Australia after a lapse of four years and renewed their former triumphs (vide New York Clipper 28th December and Sydney Morning Herald 30th October and 15th November 1877) and opened at the Queen's Theatre, Sydney, New South Wales when hundreds were unable to gain admission.

HARRY and LIZZIE BRAHAM point with pride to the fact that during their sojourn (of Seven Years) throughout the United States and the Australias that they have achieved the grandest successes and received the largest salaries of any European Artists that have ever visited either country. (NOTICE: two grand entertainments written expressly for the Brahams by the eminent composer Mr G W Hunt).

Harry went even further, taking out his own solo advertisement that read: "MR HARRY BRAHAM always refrained from feeing correspondents, and still adheres to his old motto that 'Talent will always float'". Sometimes, to gain a good review to promote a career, entertainers would pay a reporter – which Harry never did.

It is not known how these articles were sent to the newspaper, as Harry and Lizzie were en route to England at the time. It may have been that Harry had contacted his father, possibly via telegraph, and asked him to write to *The Era* – certainly, Nathaniel was so furious he wrote independently, defending them:

Mr Editor

Sir, You have, I assume, perused my advertisements in your valuable paper of the 20th and 27th inst refuting your Sydney correspondent's letter of the 13th inst., wherein he stated "Harry Braham and Lizzie Watson were a most signal failure at the Queen's Theatre Sydney, New South Wales, and Mr Bayless, the Lessee, would doubtless not be sorry when their season terminates". I need hardly point out to you the latter sentence admits the untruthfulness of the critique, and is strongly endorsed by the notice in the Sydney Morning Herald of the 30th October which denies your correspondent's statement in tote., viz:- "Harry Braham and Lizzie Watson appeared before a crowded house, and were both accorded a flattering reception". I repeat that your correspondent's letter is a mere underhanded insinuation and amounts to dishonest rhetoric and I defy him to justify his conspiracy. I trust you will look into your correspondent's next letter, and see that nothing detrimental is inserted, as you said you would have the matter thoroughly investigated. My son intends holding his caluminators liable. I am, Sir, faithfully and fraternally yours, N H Braham, 22, Redcliffe Street, South Kensington, SW 26th January, 1878.

As Harry did not usually see any need to defend their act, the criticism must have really had an effect on them, but he may also have taken action because it came at a crucial time in their transition to the UK – and could have affected their job prospects.

CHAPTER NINE
Homecoming

Unlike the clipper ships, which had to risk the high seas of Cape Horn on the return to England, the new steamships had enough power to go through the Suez Canal which had opened less than ten years previously. The *Hankow* docked in London on 13 February 1878 and, after nearly seven years abroad, Harry arrived home in style with his wife.

Harry and Lizzie went to his parents' home in South Kensington, a well-off, middle-class area. Nathaniel welcomed Lizzie warmly and Harry introduced her to his mother and to Edwin, Charles and the rest of his family. They then began a whirlwind tour of the UK including a performance at the Crystal Palace. They also appeared at the London Pavilion with two of the major stars of the stage, Arthur Lloyd and Jenny Hill (nicknamed The Vital Spark), before going to Brighton in August.

Much of the London they had known in 1871 had not changed in the last few years. Gas lighting, factories and coal fires still meant thick yellow fogs; crime and poverty were still commonplace; the rookeries still existed, and with them the dreaded workhouses. Some aspects, though, were improving. The underground railway system was well under way, creating new suburbs. New laws had been brought in giving children more of an education; bank holidays gave workers a few days paid holiday; and the new sewage system which had still been under construction when they left was now fully working and had cleaned up much of the Thames in the centre of the city. The odour from thousands of tons of horse manure still permeated the air, but the fetid smell of human effluent had more or less disappeared – and with it, the ravage of cholera.

The sewage, however, had to go somewhere and 75 million gallons was discharged twice a day down-river through new sewer outlets at Barking and Crossness, making the outskirts of London lethal. An horrific tragedy happened on 3 September when the *SS*

Princess Alice on a leisure excursion collided with the coal carrier Bywell Castle at Woolwich. The ship sank in four minutes and 650 people were killed, many of them drowning in the festering sludge. Most of the dead were women and children who had gone on a rare day-trip to the seaside.

No one in London would have been unaware of the disaster. The gruesome details of the struggle for life and the grief of those left to identify bodies covered in the smelly muck were printed in all of the newspapers, with illustrations drawn of the collision itself. Women from the workhouse were made to sew shrouds for the dead, the bodies held in makeshift mortuaries. Many of those who died were found in the saloon area when the wreck was carefully lifted – others were found miles down-river days afterwards.

Life, however, for those not touched by the tragedy went on – and so did music hall. Harry and Lizzie travelled to McFarlands Music Hall in Aberdeen for appearances the following month.

They now had an agent, Fred Gilbert, to make things easier for them, and this meant they did not have to look for work, paying him a fee to arrange bookings for them instead. The year of 1879 began again very busily with appearances in London, Dundee and Birmingham, and on 7 July Harry made his debut in Edinburgh in Moss's Theatre of Varieties in Chamber Street. *The Era* on 13 July gave this review:

> Miss Lizzie Watson who we remember, achieved great distinction as a serio-comic vocalist in this city, before her tour round the world, returns after a lengthened absence, to resume at once that high place in public esteem she held so securely before. Looking younger and sprightlier than ever, she gave a number of capital songs on Monday evening with brilliant effect to the intense delight of a crowded audience who applauded to the echo. Mr Harry Braham a newcomer, also secured the good opinion of the house, the hearty enthusiasm on his singing and his astonishing command of facial expression being warmly recognized.

They were back in Scotland again in September to appear at the opening of the New Albert Hall at Bridgeton Cross in Glasgow.

The hall had been built on the site of the Royal Albert, which was destroyed by fire in 1876. Harry and Lizzie saw that it was disappointingly rather plain on the outside, but inside it was a different matter, elaborate and comfortable with the latest furnishings. There was safety netting over the gas lights and accommodation for 2,000 people: it even had dressing rooms, a luxury usually unknown for music-hall artistes, who generally dashed to two or three halls a night in their stage outfits. The opening night was full to capacity.

Later that month, they returned to Birmingham to appear at a gala celebrating the seventeenth anniversary of the Concert Hall: special silk programmes were made for the occasion.

Whenever a significant event happened in the country, a song was usually composed and Harry was quick to pay tribute to Field Marshal Sir Garnet Joseph Wolseley (1833-1913) at a critical point in the Zulu war, when he sang 'Sir Garnet Will Show Them the Way':

At last there's good news 'bout the war in Zulu,
Where so many lives have been lost,
We've gain'd by experience dearly 'tis true
And a lesson learn'd to our cost.
But the nation has heard the news with delight
How brave Wolseley is now on his way
To take the command of our army out there
And to win he will show them the way

Chorus
So hurrah for Sir Garnet of glorious renown
The brightest of jewels in England's great crown
There'll be no disasters and no more delay
Sir Garnet will show them the way.

We all of us know how he won his great fame
By his skill and his courage true blue

On Red River 'tis said that he first made a name
And in Ashantee how his foe flew
Tho' Lord Chelmsford no doubt is a brave honest man
And Sir Bartle Frere too I daresay
They've not led our soldiers to victory yet
But Sir Garnet will show them the way.

So with hearty good will let us wish him God speed
Tis a might relief to us all
To know we've a man to depend on at need
Who will answer at duty's stern call
From the flag of Old England he'll wipe out the stain
And the Zulus for peace they will pray
For the British will beat them again and again
And Sir Garnet will show them the way.

But alas once again a message of woe
How Prince Louis Napoleon was kill'd
He was savagely stabbed by the merciless foe
Like a soldier he fell on the field
His poor noble mother with heart nearly broke
Will ever mourn that sad day
But his death will revenge with a terrible stroke
And Sir Garnet will show them the way.

Sir Garnet Joseph Wolseley was born in Dublin on 4 June 1833. He was an Anglo-Irish Officer in the army whose distinguished career saw him serve in the Crimea, Burma, the Indian mutiny, China, Africa and Canada. He was involved in the 'Red River Rebellion' in Canada when Louis Riel led a rebellion of the indigenous Métis people of the Red River Settlement, who were becoming marginalised and being taken over by Protestant

The sheet-music cover for Sir Garnet Will Show Them the Way, 'sung with great success by Sam Torr and Harry Braham'

whites. Riel became leader of a provisional government and formed a bill of rights with some Canadian supporters for a union, when a minority of ultra Pro-Canadian supporters formed a plot against the provisional government to take it over. Thomas Scott, who had been employed as a surveyor by the Canadian government and had been arrested with a number of others by Riel at Fort Garry, was executed when he refused to yield to Riel's demands. When news of his death reached Ontario, Wolseley was despatched to seize the

Fort from Riel and arrest him as a murderer: Riel fled but was later captured and executed for treason against the Canadian government. The bill of rights which he had drawn up for the Métis people led to the creation of the province of Manitoba and was absorbed into the Manitoba Act of 1870 which secured them land and language rights.

Wolseley then organised the expedition for the colonisation of the Gold Coast in Africa, leading to conflict with the Ashanti people. This campaign of only two months in 1873 led to him being given the freedom of the City of London and the sword of honour. Although not much involved in the Zulu war, he was ordered to take over from Lord Chelmsford who was commanding it and who had had a crushing defeat at the hands of the Zulus at the battle of Islandlwana, after Chelmsford's friend – Sir Bartle Frere – had forced a war with King Cetshwayo. Chelmsford then defeated the Zulus at the Battle of Ulundi before Wolseley arrived, though he did set up a temporary peace settlement.

Prince Louis Napoleon, who is mentioned in the song, was the only son of Napoleon Bonaparte III and Empress Eugenie, and was killed in battle in the Zulu war. Wolseley became commander in chief of the forces from 1895 to 1900 and his reputation for efficiency coined a Victorian saying "Everything's all Sir Garnet" meaning "all is in order".

By the age of 29, Harry had seen and experienced a world most artistes could only dream about. Work was hard, but rewarding. He could not know that his life was about to fall apart.

CHAPTER TEN

Heartbreak

Wherever Harry and Lizzie toured, newspapers were loud in their praise of their act and in March 1880 they travelled back up to Glasgow, known as the second city of the Empire for its size and industry, though the riches of the 'tobacco lords' and the large shipyards had failed to make their mark in the East End of the city. The Trongate was one of the worst areas, where brothels, pubs and slums predominated. There were a

Britannia Music Hall, Glasgow, pictured in the 1880s

number of music halls there, which provided some amusement away from the other 'entertainments' on offer and where women and children could go and vent their frustrations at any act unfortunate enough not to be accepted on stage.

Harry and Lizzie appeared first at Browns Music Hall and then at the Britannia – the first time Harry had been on the bill there. Lizzie approached the Britannia with some trepidation. She knew that the manager, H T Rossborough, might not take too kindly to her return – ten years previously, she had taken him to court. She had claimed unfair dismissal when he refused to pay her after she came off-stage and refused to go back on, saying she was ill. Rossborough counter-claimed by stating she had breached her contract. The court had ruled in his favour, however – something that might have made it easier for her to go back to him.

Would Rossborough forgive her? They were contracted for a week from 4 April. Their success had led to this job, but would her reputation as a troublemaker ruin it for them? The audience was also notorious for its intolerance of any act it deemed not good enough: rivets from the shipyards, rotten fruit, and manure were known to be thrown, and young boys aimed with deadly accuracy from the balcony in a hall with no toilet facilities.

Luckily, Lizzie seemed to re-establish her relationship with Rossborough and – together with the other artistes appearing there that week including negroist Tom Clegg, ballad singer Bella Collins, variety entertainers Messrs Pullas and Cusick and violinist Barry Wilson – Lizzie and Harry went down a storm.

Harry and Lizzie's schedule was unrelenting and their career was going from strength to strength, but behind the scenes, cracks in their marriage were beginning to appear. From various articles, it is clear that Lizzie had a hot temper, and though there are few articles describing Harry's temperament, he was later to fall out with his family after a row, so any marital arguments may well have been lively! It will never fully be known how or why their marriage fell apart, but there is one shocking truth about Lizzie which, if Harry did discover it, would have totally destroyed their relationship. Lizzie was not a widow at all – her husband, Henry Hemingway, was still alive.

The circumstances of Lizzie's parting from Hemingway are not known. Had she already separated from him when she found love with Richard Ramsden? Census records show she had stayed at the Union Hotel in Dundee with Ramsden a few months prior to them going to Australia in 1871. Was the emigration truly to better their careers, or was she leaving the country to escape from Hemingway?

After leaving the army, Hemingway had become a clerk in the music-hall business and wrote articles for various newspapers. It would have been fairly easy for him to find out which halls Lizzie and Harry were working in, and – through gossip – to discover that they were 'married'. In Australia and America they were billed as 'The Brahams', but in the UK their names were billed separately with Lizzie returning to her theatrical name, and it would not have been so obvious. It is possible that he saw one of their performances and confronted Lizzie or even Harry. If this was the reason for the split, Harry's reaction to this stunning revelation can only be imagined.

It may have been that, after seven years away from England, she thought sufficient time had elapsed for it not to matter, and that it would be safe to return with Harry. Maybe just the stress of living a lie, or professional jealousies between the two working so close together, had caused some arguments? Could it even be that she really thought Hemingway was dead when she married Harry – only for him to reappear like an awful ghost from the past?

In all their performances so far, Harry and Lizzie were on the same bill, with both doing solo performances and sometimes a duet. In September they were still appearing together, but then their work pattern seemed to change.

Harry was at the Royal London on 10 October 1880 performing solo and Lizzie was not on the bill. He had a lengthy performance that night. One of the comic songs poked fun at the well-known animosity between Conservative leader Benjamin Disraeli, the 1st Earl of Beaconsfield, who had been defeated in the general election earlier in the year by the Liberal William Ewart Gladstone, but *The Era* review felt other aspects of his performance hinted at some personal difficulties:

Mr Harry Braham pleased the audience with his

evidently well-studied performances. He sang a song in which Beaconsfield and Gladstone were represented as "Rival Showmen", and after that gave an impersonation of an unlovely female, who sings "My first husband was a nice young man", his next character was that of a so-called "Major in the Salvation Army". He gave, too, specimens of the singing of an Irishman, a Hibernian lass, and a Negro. Finally he transformed himself into "The Wild Man of The Woods". This act elicited very hearty applause.

On 21 November he was performing again at the Sun Music Hall in London and *The Era* gave this review: "Harry Braham, a clever and amusing artist, personated a widow whose first husband according to her own account, was a nice young man; appeared as a captain in the Salvation Army; and wound up by an extraordinary imitation of the grimaces of a monkey".

Was this song a disguised reference to Lizzie and Hemingway who, although not in the Salvation Army, had originally been an artillery officer? At this time the Salvation Army was treated with contempt for introducing temperance, which had a negative impact on music halls which depended on sale of liquor. Perhaps this song was also an attempt to show his own feelings?

It wasn't long, though, before Harry and Lizzie were back performing together, first at Garcia's in Manchester where they appeared in the burlesque of 'Naughty Cupid' and then at the Theatre Royal in Edinburgh for the Christmas season. As they had an agent, they would have been contracted for these performances, so any personal difficulties would have to have been set aside.

There was no let up at the beginning of 1881. In February they were at the Prince of Wales Concert Hall in Nottingham for a benefit in aid of the Mission School, followed by Paul's Hall of Varieties in Leicester in March when Harry sang one of his most popular songs 'I'm a lawyer, my name is Marks'.

The census in April showed Harry living at the family home in Redcliffe Street in London while Lizzie was staying in Kingston upon Hull, in a Cambridge Street lodging house along with William Seaward, a comedian/negro delineator. Was this due to separate work commitments, or an ominous sign?

Harry and Lizzie's triumph the previous year at the Britannia in Glasgow had secured them another contract: they played for a week there before leaving for engagements at Birmingham and Leeds. Harry then went on to the Harp Music Hall in Ramsgate alone and Lizzie re-joined him a week later. The following two-week engagement must have been a great strain, for after eight tumultuous years performing to thousands of people, in so many places in the world, from the elite of society to the roughnecks in the goldfields, the end came for their professional and private life as a highly successful partnership. Did they have one final major row, or had they perhaps already decided to break up after the contract finished?

Lizzie did not take long to go back on the road and by the end of July she was at Foresters Music Hall in London before travelling to McFarlands in Aberdeen, where she was a massive success with arguably the most famous singer/songwriter of the period, Arthur Lloyd.

Lizzie had always been the more dominant partner with a wealth of experience behind her, and had been, until now, more well-known than Harry. As if to prove that nothing had changed – professionally at least – she took out a large advertisement in *The Era* confirming her success in Aberdeen. She then embarked on an extensive tour for the rest of the year, that took in Dundee, Dublin, Edinburgh, Glasgow and Birmingham.

CHAPTER ELEVEN
Going Solo

Harry returned to his parents in London: they were probably aware of his problems, and were very supportive. He had always been confident in his own talent, having had success before he met Lizzie, but the split seemed either to have knocked this self-belief or severely traumatised him, as it took him nearly a month to get back to some sort of normality and begin working again.

He appeared first at the South London Palace of Varieties on 20 August, where he remained for a couple of weeks, and then at the Queens Palace London from September including a benefit for Fred Coyne, one of the Lions Comiques, with male impersonator Vesta Tilley and minstrel Charles Sutton on the same bill. Of these Vesta Tilley (Matilda Alice Powles 1864-1952) was the most famous: as a star in the UK and USA for 30 years, she was viewed as a symbol of female independence. She and her husband, a music-hall entrepreneur named Walter de Frece, were to reach even more prominence when they began a recruitment drive in the Great War. Walter was knighted as a result of his contribution to the war and charity work and later became an MP. Now Lady de Frece, Vesta left show-business and they retired to Monte Carlo. As a male impersonator she was careful to retain her femininity and was always fashionable off stage.

Harry revived the 'Salvation Army' song on 1 October at the Queens and appeared there during November. In December he was at the Temple of Varieties London with another of the Lion Comiques, The Great Vance.

At this time, songwriters did not retain the copyright on their songs – artistes paid them a couple of guineas for a song, which then became the singer's copyright to do with as they wished. It was considered the greatest sin to sing another artiste's song without their permission.

Most singers owned copyrights to their songs and Harry was no exception – among others he had the copyright of 'The Old Village Blacksmith Shop'. In August 1881, he had stated that he would sue anyone who sung it without his permission, but by December he was offering to sell the singing rights. Whether this decision was prompted because of what happened with Lizzie is unknown: as part of the lyrics are set in Ireland, it is possible:

Some folks like to visit strange lands and their ways
While some go to Paris or Rome
But the spot I love best and am longing to see
Is in Ireland, my own village home.
'Tis there that I spent many hours when a boy
And 'tis there that I often would stop
To watch the old blacksmith displaying his power
In the old village blacksmith's shop

Chorus

Dang, bang, bang, falls the hammer on the anvil
All day long at the door I would stop
Listening to the music made by honest toil
In the old village blacksmith's shop

'Tis there, when a boy, that my schoolmates and I
Would stand 'round the old smithy fire
And watch the old smith as he swung his huge sled
And envy his muscular power
And then the old man would pause in his work
And his ponderous hammer he'd stop
To talk to us kindly and call us his boys
In the old village blacksmiths shop

'Tis often I think of the days that are gone
When to the old smith I'd go
And to help the old man on a box I would stand
And with pleasure his bellows I'd blow
But the old man has gone to his last resting place
And no more at the door I can stop
To watch the sparks fly from the fire to the sky
In the old village blacksmith's shop.

Harry's songs were often topical: The Danger Signal was written in response to the death of a signalman on the London to Southampton railway line

Harry's songs, as with those of most music-hall artistes, were always topical. His song 'The Danger Signal', for which he composed the music, was written in reaction to the tragic story in May 1881 of railway signalman Samuel Gunner. Gunner was working at his signal box and had operated the red signal at Sheerwater, near Woking. A mail train from Southampton to London stopped on seeing it. When the signal did not change for some time, the passengers started to call out, asking what was wrong. The fireman of the steam-train got out to investigate and found poor Mr Gunner dead in the signal box, apparently from a heart attack. If he had died while the signal was on green, there might have been a catastrophic crash.

*The morning was fine as a Signalman went
To his post on the South Western line.
Little thinking that ere that bright May day had pass'd
His post he would have to resign.
But on comes a train 'tis the London day mail
To stop pages mostly a stranger
It dashes along 'till it nears Gunner's box
When 'tis stopp'd by the signal of danger.*

*What's wrong was the cry, but they got no reply,
That silence seem'd stranger and stranger,
They sought him and found Gunner dead at his post,
With the signal hand pointing to danger.*

In the early months of 1882, Harry was still mainly appearing at various halls in London including the Temple Hall of Varieties, the Star, and the South London Palace, but he could not have failed to have seen where Lizzie was appearing, as the newspaper *The Era* was the only paper for music-hall artistes to keep up-to-date with their profession – indeed, it was a matter of pride to be seen with the paper because it showed you to be a 'professional'.

If Lizzie looked for Harry's name, did she feel emotional? She had, after all, spent eight years with him. She would be able to see he was having his own successes and on 15 April he appeared in the annual comedy festival at the Great St James Hall in Manchester.

The music-hall world always came to the aid of one of their own when help was needed, and on 22 April he starred with many other well-known artistes including Marie Loftus, all of whom gave their services free at the Town Hall, Shoreditch, for a benefit for the songwriter and comic vocalist Arthur Lloyd, who had just been made bankrupt when his venture in opening the Shakespeare Music Hall in Glasgow failed. Lizzie was not on the bill.

In July, Harry appeared at another benefit – this time at the Cambridge for Nelly Power who had sustained a severe head injury during a performance in Birmingham. Nelly (1854-1887) was a very popular singer and actress who mimicked George Leybourne and other 'dandies' and who was also in pantomime with Vesta Tilley. The song 'The Boy I Love is up in the Gallery' which was made famous by Marie Lloyd was originally written for Nelly. After appearances at the Oxford in London, Harry's confidence was further boosted by being booked in Paris for a month: it must have brought back memories of his 1870s song 'Parisian 'Arry'!

At the end of November, Harry was performing at the London Pavilion, Piccadilly, when he discovered that Harry Rickards was back in England and had been contracted to appear at the same theatre. Rickards had appeared at the Bush Street Theatre in San Francisco for a couple of months while Harry and Lizzie were appearing in their lengthy engagement at the Belle Union back in 1874, and they may well have met at that time. As the two of them met up again, they would undoubtedly have talked about his parting with Lizzie and they may well have reconciled any differences. In fact, years later, Harry was asked to write Rickard's obituary for the *New York Clipper.*

Harry also started appearing with another artiste – Lily Grey – and starred with her many times over the next couple of years. Conversations between the two could well have been very interesting, involving a very different Harry Braham (see Afterword).

By 1883, he had changed agents and was under contract to Ambrose Maynard. He was increasingly getting admiration for his act, and building a good reputation by appearing on the bill with artistes such as George Leybourne, Charles Coburn, Vesta Tilley and Arthur Lloyd, and being asked for personal appearances at private functions. One such private function was for the Marquess of Queensberry, after which he was given an elaborate walking stick. The stick was made of applewood and the handle, in the shape of an eagle's claw, made of solid gold, its talon holding an Oriental bloodstone the size of a hen's egg and the claws tipped with a precious stone. This stick was acquired by a major collector – J Charles Davis of the Palace Theatre in New York – in April 1889. Whether Harry gave it as a gift or whether the collector bought it from Harry is also unknown; because of Harry's lifestyle, he may have thought it too precious to

Something Like This, part of Harry's Masks and Faces performance, 1887

keep on his person. The Marquess of Queensberry, John Sholto Douglas, was famous for lending his name to boxing's 'Marquess of Queensberry Rules' and was a controversial figure, alienating his family by selling the ancestral home in Scotland and feuding with his two sons, Francis – rumoured to have a homosexual relationship with Liberal Prime Minister Richard Primrose – and Alfred ('Bosie'), whose affair with Oscar Wilde he tried to end by writing the word "sodomite" on a visiting card at Wilde's club.

Performance schedules were very tight and necessitated travelling between two or three music halls a night for about a ten-minute slot at each. Although this meant artistes could do their same act time and time again, knowing that audiences would always see it afresh, it was exhausting. If the halls were nearby, the artistes would walk or run in costume, or more likely hail a carriage to take them to their next engagement.

This had its own hazards, relying on horses in very busy, dirty, uneven roads. On 3 February 1883, Harry was anxious to get to his next engagement at the Marylebone Music Hall. He hailed a carriage to get from the Trocadero when suddenly the carriage jarred, or the horse shied. The coachman desperately tried to calm the horse and control it, but nothing could stop the carriage overturning. Harry was thrown out and landed on the road badly shaken and bruised. Getting to the Marylebone was out of the question, and he had to take a couple of days off to recover.

Harry was probably still sore on 8 February at his next appearance, at the South London Palace, when a drama occurred during a performance of one of the acts which could have had disastrous consequences. Shouts of alarm could be heard when a youth dropped a piece of clothing onto one of the gaslit chandeliers near the private boxes and it caught fire. A quick-thinking member of the audience managed to retrieve it, using an umbrella, and dowsed the flames: there were sighs of relief and applause from everyone in the hall – and the entertainment was able to continue.

During the rest of the year, Harry continued his demanding schedule, appearing once more in Paris before returning to London. On Bank Holiday, 11 August, he appeared at the Oxford Theatre of Varieties in Brighton – which was becoming, with its new railway links, a favourite place for a day out from London. He was back on the music-hall circuit until December, when he appeared at a benefit for The Great Vance at the Sun in Knightsbridge, with Bessie Bonehill – a male impersonator who inspired Vesta Tilley, and who widely toured the USA after Tony Pastor invited her to appear at his theatre – and Harry Rickards on the same bill. It was on that stage, just a few years later, on Boxing Day 1888, when The Great Vance was to drop dead just as he finished his performance.

At Christmas Harry appeared at the Canterbury, and at Lusby's Summer and Winter Palace with George Leybourne. Leybourne and The Great Vance (born Alfred Peck Stevens in 1839) were rivals, appearing on stage as 'swells' dressed in top hat and tails. They vied with each other to get the best 'drinking song' and were known as Lions Comiques. Leybourne obtained the song 'Champagne Charlie', which then became his theme song – he was given free champagne to popularise the song and unsurprisingly eventually died an alcoholic.

In 1884 Harry was touring, visiting Southampton, Plymouth, Aberdeen, Preston, Nottingham and Liverpool. In towns and cities all over the UK, music-hall artistes stayed in the same boarding houses and guest-houses, which catered for their particular needs. Harry and Lizzie's paths may well have crossed many times. Up until now they had been apart professionally, but on 17 May their engagements clashed for the first time when they were both on the bill at Paul's Theatre of Varieties in Leicester. *The Era*, in its review, said: "Harry Braham is making a very big hit with new songs, Miss Lizzie Watson is also very much applauded". While making no mention of their prior relationship, the better review seemed to be for Harry this time. It must have been a difficult engagement.

In October, Harry appeared at the Alhambra in Belfast for the first time, and was joined for a couple of shows by the man who became the best-known music-hall artiste of them all – Dan Leno. Leno had been a child artiste with his family, and had just started his solo career that year in London. A former champion clog dancer, he went on to be one of the most highly paid comedians in the world, best known as a pantomime dame and comedian who created characters which epitomised working-class life. He so impressed

King Edward VII at Sandringham that he became known as 'The King's Jester' – he later succumbed to alcoholism and a mental breakdown at the age of 43.

One of Harry's hobbies on a rare break was riding in a dog cart – a one-horse carriage – but on 23 May 1885 he was thrown when the horse shied: he was lucky to escape with a severe shaking, though this time his injuries kept him off work for a week. He received a lot of letters from friends and well-wishers and he entered an advertisement in *The Era* thanking them: 'Mr Harry Braham begs to return thanks for the many kind letters of inquiry after his health; progressing favourably'.

There was not much time to recover before he was working again: at the Welsh Harp in Hendon, Collins Music Hall in Islington and the Temple of Varieties in Hammersmith. He had, by this time, changed agents again and was now on the books of the most powerful agent in the business: Hugh Jay Didcott.

In June he performed at Folly's in Manchester before going to the Gaiety in Sauchiehall Street, Glasgow. In July he returned to Paris, but was back later that month at the Harp in Ramsgate: it could not have been pleasant, as it was the last theatre he had appeared in with Lizzie before they split up. He would not have had time to get sad or depressed though – work kept him extremely busy, with rehearsals between shows and it was not long before he was off to London again, performing at the Paragon and Canterbury.

In October, he appeared back at the Gaiety in Glasgow with the darling of the Scottish music hall, Glasgow-born Marie Loftus, a full-figured lady who became widely known as a buxom principal boy in pantomime and as a singer of both risqué and love songs in the UK and USA, earning over £100 a week at the height of her fame in the 1890s. In 1894, while appearing at the Britannia in Glasgow, she bought 150 pairs of strong boots to be donated to the poorest children. She was also on the bill with Harry at the Star music hall in Watson Street, Glasgow Cross (originally Arthur Lloyd's failed Shakespeare Theatre) which was, together with the Britannia, one of the halls notorious for a hard-to-please audience. This time the audience booed and jeered his performance. However, either he eventually won his audience over or changed his act, because when

Harry's song, co-written with J S Haydon, extolling the virtues of Burnaby the Brave, the first media idol

he reappeared at the Star the following week he got a good review. From Glasgow he took the train, crisscrossing the country by the various railway companies: on 9 November he was at the Amphitheatre in Portsmouth, before travelling to the Days Concert Hall in Birmingham.

When he could, Harry composed the music for his songs, asking only for lyric writers. He collaborated with J S Haydon on 'Burnaby The Brave' in tribute to Frederick Gustavus Burnaby, an extremely popular idol known for writing books about his daredevil travels on horseback in far-off places and for his feats of bravery as a soldier. He had been killed earlier in the year in hand-to-hand combat at the Battle of Abu Klea:

> *Across the plains of Egypt and the desert of Soudan,*
> *Amid Old England's sons of war,*
> *Rode one brave Englishman.*
> *A better soldier ne'er drew sword,*
> *Upon the tented field, prepared to prove this motto true,*
> *"We die but never yield!"*
> *A British hero, staunch and true,*
> *Has found a soldier's grave,*

He died as British heroes do,
This dear old land to save

He e're was foremost in the van,
He ne're knew taint of fear
He fought as Britons only can
He heard that British cheer
But ere the shout of Victory
Rose o'er the savage yell,
His blood had stained the desert sand
Our hero fighting fell.

Still onward pressed our little band
The foemen strove in vain
For Britain's sons with dauntless hearts
Avenge their comrade slain
On that rude field at Abu-Klea
They made a soldier's grave
And in that grave our hero lies
Fred Burnaby the Brave.

Burnaby (born in Bedford on 3 March 1842) stood 6'4" tall with a 47-inch chest. He was immensely strong, being able to break horseshoes and bend pokers around disagreeable dinner guests' necks for fun. His strength was such that when a couple of officers led two ponies into his room as a joke, he picked up a pony under each arm and took them outside. He could speak seven languages, and travelled to the most inhospitable places on earth such as Uzbekistan, where it was so cold his beard froze solid and broke off. He wrote a string of bestsellers about his travels to places such as Turkey and Russia, including an autobiography running to seventeen editions – he also founded the magazine *Vanity Fair*, and led the Household Cavalry and the Turkish Army. In 1882 he became the first person

The sheet-music for Kiss When You Can

to cross the English Channel in a hot air balloon; he also survived typhus and arsenic poisoning. He was dashing, debonair and the first media idol, as mass newspapers started to be published thanks to cheaper printing presses. Papers like *The Graphic*, *Daily Mail* and *Illustrated News* kept readers enthralled by his exploits. Burnaby souvenirs could be bought, such as posters, toby jugs, and playing cards. He even had his own sponsorship deal with 'Cockle's Cure All Ointments'. Recognising the early signs of middle age and determining to die a hero's death befitting his image, he joined the attempt to rescue General Gordon at Khartoum: during an ambush by Sudanese warriors at Al Klea, he broke through the ranks and rode out alone, and was killed by a spear. Queen Victoria was said to have fainted at the news of his death.

In 1886, Harry continued his exhausting performing schedule, going to Birkenhead, Brighton, Yarmouth, Manchester, Liverpool and Ramsgate. In July he appeared in Deacons Music Hall in London with Dan Leno and Marie Loftus, and again with Leno in September at the famous Alhambra. For one evening he took Leno's place, but his act on that occasion was not up to his usual standard and he was criticised in the press for his lame performance.

Meanwhile Lizzie was living in Bristol using her married name – Eliza Hemingway. Perhaps she had gone back to her husband? She was having money problems and owed debt-collector Abraham Collins £40. Apart from a couple of appearances in 1888, there does not seem to be any further record of her appearing in the UK. In the early 1890s she was working in vaudeville in America, but there her trail ends until her death on 17 February 1913 on her farm in Richmond, Indiana, presumably her home in retirement.

CHAPTER TWELVE
Harry Turns Legit

Harry was under contract to Edward Colley from September 1886 but then returned to Hugh Didcott in 1887. His act, 'Masks and Faces', was judged good enough for a solo tour and Didcott arranged for him to go to America. It would be strange returning to New York by himself and – determined to make it a success – he rehearsed new characters long and hard. He boarded the steamship *Germanic* at Liverpool on New Year's Day 1887. One of the famous White Star Line, she was one of the fastest sailing ships to cross the Atlantic.

As he neared New York, the first sight that greeted him was the brand new figure of the Statue of Liberty which had been dedicated just a couple of months previously, towering majestically over the city. The last time he saw it was when only her arm with the torch was displayed in Madison Square Park, to encourage donations. It had looked huge then, but now it seemed small in comparison to the statue itself. The view of this magnificent gift from France must have struck the passengers with awe and wonder as they steamed into port.

Harry performed in his old friend Tony Pastor's new theatre in Tammany Hall on 14th Street at Union Square. The theatre boasted electric light, plush box drapes and red carpeting and was considered the height of theatrical entertainment where the whole family could go to, due to Tony's insistence on clean humour and high-class artistes.

The tour of the theatres in New York was a fantastic success and Harry did not return to the UK until June for his vacation, arriving amid the excitement and patriotic fervour of Queen Victoria's Golden Jubilee. He wrote a couple of articles for the *New York Clipper*, the first of which (published on 4 July 1887) gives an insight into just how vibrant the theatrical scene was in London at that time:

Oh The Jubilee! In fact that is the cry everywhere. People have it on the brain. London is full yes crowded and entertainments are booming. Italian Opera at 3 Opera Houses at Her Majesty's Middle Hauk at Drury Lane and Mme Alban at Covent Garden.

Things theatrical are not out of the hunt. Charles Warner in Held by the Enemy has left the Princess and is now in full blast at the Vaudeville, if ever "Charley" goes to America he will be a big go.

Mrs Bernard Beere is scoring in "As in a Looking Glass" at the Comique, J L Took finishes his season July 9 and then John Clayton takes possession of his theatre. Mrs John Wood is still at the Court Theatre (This theatre is shortly to be torn down). Agnes Hewitt (Mrs Lytton Sothern) is still manageress of the Olympic where The Golden Band is being played. George Barrett, J P Barnett and J L Graham are in the Carl. Speaking of the Haymarket Theatre the new lessee is Beerbohm Tree who takes The Red Lamp from The Comedy in Sep. Mr Tree is a finished artist Ruddygore is still being played to packed houses at the Savoy. Miss Ulma scoring all the time. So much for the theatres. Buffalo Bill is the lion of the season, and it is really impossible for one to get a conveyance from the west end afternoon or evening (especially Jubilee week) Nate Salsbury and Mr Cody have seemingly endeared themselves to all classes of the British public. The music halls are not left in the cold. The Pavilion, The Trocadero, Metropolitan, Canterbury, Alhambra are nightly turning people away. House Full is the cry everywhere. Many American performers are playing at the London Halls – John Morris, Sweeney and Ryland, Carl Hertz, Wilson Brothers, Orville Parker, Fish and Ralston, Rowe and Athol, St Felix Sisters, Harry La Rose, Lydia Yemans, Major Newes, Sisters Richmond, Ida Morris and others. Nellie Wilson lately from Australia is a very clever soubrette and dancer. She may visit your shores this fall – a really good card for variety managers. The childrens Jubilee fete held in Hyde Park and visited by the Queen was catered for by Hugh Jay Didcott (who is by now surnamed The Royal Caterer complimented by the Queen and the Prince of Wales. Mr Didcott may bring to America an old English pantomime company the same as Londoners are used to at the Drury Lane but with the Alhambra ballet thrown in. I believe Mr Didcott's manager is now in New York looking after a big theatre. Tony Pastor and his wife held a grand reception at Morley's Hotel Tuesday last. Tony has already made heaps of friends and I hardly tell is seeing the sights. I saw him the other night, I said well Tony how do you like the Old Country? "Harry I am quite stuck with it: by Gemenetti it is a great country". I saw Marshall P Wilder the other day he tells me that his concerts have been catching on big – I hear that George Keogh (Mrs Langtry's manager) has bought through her agents a large green diamond weighing 35 carats and valued at fifty thousand dollars, it originally belonged to the Queen of Onde and was brought to this country at the time of the Indian Mutiny. Flags are waving everywhere today July 4 I hear from good authority that there are one hundred and fifty thousand Americans in London.

Harry took the opportunity to see a number of plays during the couple of months he was in London, including the play 'Civil War' at the Gaiety, in which he saw the beautiful Mrs James Brown Potter, an American socialite who had become a well-known actress. Harry managed to talk to Marshall P Wilder, a dwarf who had refused offers from showmen such as P T Barnum to be in a sideshow, defied the critics and gone on stage. He had since become a Royal Family favourite with his comic songs and monologues (the Prince of Wales went to see him around 20 times) and was in between sell-out shows.

All too soon, he had to leave the buzz of London behind, arriving back in New York on 29 August on board the *Arizona*, the Germanic's main competitor for the Blue Riband.

His own act had shown audiences his ability for characterisation, and he was now approached to act in a play. For a vaudeville comic vocalist, it was extremely rare to be judged talented enough to transfer to the legitimate theatre circuit.

'Hoodman Blind' was a melodrama written by Henry Arthur Jones and Wilson Barrett. Its plot was a variation on 'Othello', with murder over money, revenge of a spurned lover and the mistaken identity of two half-sisters, identical in looks. One is kind and faithful, married to the hero and saving him from alcohol and drugs; the other is a thief and vagabond who is paid to bring the hero down by playing the part of her sister and making him jealous, when seeing her in the arms of another. Harry was engaged to play the part of Ben Chibbles, a kindly blacksmith, friend of the hero of the story, Ben Yeulett. He made his debut on 19 September at the People's Theatre in New York. The contract would only last if he was deemed good enough and the play a success, and for the rehearsals he did not get paid. This was a gamble: he was used to his own speciality act, but it paid off. Harry played Ben Chibbles for an incredible 35 weeks, both in New York and on tour.

In March 1888 Harry and the company were playing at the Grand Opera House in New York when he experienced the worst blizzard in the city's history. An unusually mild spell had led to heavy rainfall, when a snow-storm and high winds struck. Within hours, 40-feet high drifts covered houses and the whole city came to a standstill. It was cut off from the outside world when the newly introduced telegraph poles and wires were brought down, covering the streets in a maze of danger from electric shock. People froze trying to reach shelter, theatres were shut, and Harry would have been forced – as many others were – to stay indoors, watching helplessly as the snow battered the city for a day and a half. When the snow stopped and the winds eased, the full horrific effects were felt as the snow melted, causing flooding. Over 200 corpses of people and animals were found where they had fallen victim to exposure. The city was totally unprepared for the devastation and the major transport disruption caused as all the trains were powered by cables: horses and carriages were stuck or abandoned to their fate. A few years later, Harry would have seen the beginnings of the first subway which in part came about because of what had become known as the Great White Hurricane.

While Harry was playing at the Opera House, Steele Mackaye – whose work he had admired for some time – had put on his own play about the French Revolution, 'Paul Kauvar' which was running at the Standard Theatre. Mackaye, who had already seen Harry's acting, then signed him to play Citizen Dodolphe Potin for the next theatre season, starting in September.

After a visit back to Britain to spend time with his family – and do some theatre work when he could – Harry began rehearsals for 'Paul Kauvar' and his portrayal of Potin earned him praise from the theatre critics. The *New York Mirror* stated that he "gave a decidedly comic exposition of Potin". Mackaye had originally entitled the play 'Anarchy', possibly inspired by what he saw as the unfair trial and execution of the 'Chicago Anarchists' in 1887, a group of eight strikers who had been found guilty without sufficient evidence of throwing a bomb which had killed a number of policemen during a rally campaigning for an eight-hour working day, in Haymarket Square Chicago. Of the eight, four had been hanged and one committed suicide. The name was changed to avoid any charge that he may have used this for advertising.

Harry left the play in January but still showed his versatility when he appeared on 16 February 1889 for three weeks at Koster and Bials Theatre in New York as Caesar in the burlesque 'McAnthony and Chloe Pottra'.

More importantly, later the same year his performances came to the notice of the most famous comic actor and manager of the day, William Henry Crane, better known as W H Crane. He numbered among his friends and fans, well-known actors and various senators: President Grover Cleveland was a personal friend, Crane sometimes taking vacations on the President's private yacht with him.

Crane was putting together a small company of talented performers, one of whom was the actress Georgie Drew Barrymore – a member of the Barrymore acting dynasty – and asked Harry to join. To be contracted for the season by Crane was the epitome of comedic acting success: he had gained confidence performing

Harry as Baron Ling Ching in the stageplay The Senator

On Stage with W H Crane in The Senator, 1890

in plays through his parts of Ben Chibbles and Potin, but this was more of a challenge – he would be expected to learn and rehearse different plays running at the same time. He had had to learn many monologues for his own act, but this was entirely different and he had not memorised many lines simultaneously for some time. Crane obviously had faith in him and this appointment was crucial for him to be fully acknowledged as an actor. With an excellent memory, he soon adapted and became a valued member of the troupe.

The first play he was involved in was a short-lived farce, 'On Probation', in which Harry played Benjamin Cox, a Cockney traveler: his performance was well received but the play was not critically acclaimed.

Crane then introduced what was to be his most successful and long-running play. It was written by David D Lloyd and finished by Sydney Rosenfeld after Lloyd's sudden death. 'The Senator' was about social and political life in The White House. The central character, Senator Hannibal Rivers, was played by Crane. It was based on the historical events of the war against the British in 1812 and the burning of the American privateer General Armstrong by the

British fleet. The story was merged into the claim for compensation brought before Congress by the owners of the ship.

Harry played the part of Baron Ling Ching, the Chinese Secretary of Legation, learning American manners and customs, taking notes of what Rivers said and did – and reciting them at the same time. Harry's portrayal of the character became well known as a classic piece of comedy impersonation, and was talked about in theatrical circles long after his death. Apart from his ability to play various roles with different accents, the fact that Harry could compose music also came in useful, when he wrote some of the accompanying melodies.

This part, in particular, was one of the main reasons he was engaged by Crane each season.

'The Senator' became so popular that for the next five years it was played in addition to many other productions, one of them the popular play 'The Balloon', in which Harry played a doctor's servant, who keeps coming into scenes at the wrong time with hilarious results. Crane played the part of the doctor, who escapes in a balloon after believing he had poisoned his fiancée's lover.

Harry was now becoming very well-known and his image appeared on the front page of the *New York Clipper* on 8 February 1890 along with this article:

> The original of the portrait we present this week was born of theatrical parents in London, Eng. in 1850. Mr. Braham commenced his professional career when quite young, playing small parts on the York and Lincoln circuit with a travelling company. When only 15 he visited Australia, playing Melbourne, Sydney, Adelaide and Brisbane, and travelling all through the interior. He also visited New Zealand, and had a most successful tour of New Caledonia where he met Mr. Rochfort and Oliver Pain. Mr. Braham's last appearance in Sydney N.S.W. was in conjunction with the late Chas Young and Johnny Hydes, he next visited China, Japan, India, and Ceylon. giving the entertainment alone with the aid of a pianist and agent. Mr. Braham,

with his monologue entitled The Heads of Peculiar People We Meet, is still well known in those Eastern countries. From India he visited Aden, Suez and Port Said and then made a pleasant trip through the Holy Land, spending a week in Jerusalem. The next point of interest were the Pyramids, Alexandria and Cairo. Then, taking boat he sailed down the Mediterranean Sea to Malta, Gibraltar and once again to London. He next played all the provincial towns of England, Ireland and Scotland. In Birmingham he played at the Theatre Royal in one of the most gorgeous pantomimes of modern times "The Fair one with the Golden Locks". Mr. Braham appearing as Count Plentipon, and as Bob Harding in the drama of "The Old Toll House". The next season he played for J. H. Howard of the Theatre Royal, Edinburgh, Scot., appearing in the pantomime of "Aladdin". Mr. Braham was Clorinda, one of the sisters. His successful burlesque of "Pygmalion and his Gal-a-dear", he playing Gal-a-dear and had a great run during which Paris, Berlin, Brussels, St Petersburg, Turkey, Madrid, Lisbon and many European cities were visited. Mr. Braham next visited California, Australia and South Africa, going up (unreadable) ... of Kimberly, and purchasing many gems of the first water. The trip from California to New York he has accomplished on many occasions, playing in all the cities of note in the Union. Mr. Braham has been shipwrecked on four occasions, first on The Queen of The Thames which ran ashore on the African coast. He lost all his possessions but got ashore safe and sound. The next wreck was the Rangoon that went ashore at Ceylon. Mr. Braham was more fortunate this time, saving a trunk. The next was the Tartar going from Auckland, N.Z. to Frisco. She ran on a coral reef in the night, and all the passengers worked for their lives and threw overboard the cargo they were all delighted to arrive at Honolulu H. I. and stayed there some time, giving performances three times a week.

King Kalakaua patronised the Hawaiian Theatre all the time. The last disaster was the Gutenberg. She was wrecked in Torres Straits Northern Aus. Five hundred souls perished, Mr. Braham being one of the few that got ashore safely. Mr. Braham has played in London for some years. In 1887 he again visited the United States, being specially engaged for the part of Ben Chibbles in "Hoodman Blind". The next season he played Dodolphe Potin in "Paul Kauvar". The present season he is with W. H. Crane. He has appeared in that gentleman's repertory as David, the Doctor's Boy in "The Balloon"; Isadore in "Papa Perrichon"; Benjamin Cocks in "On Probation" and last but not least creating the character of the Chinaman Baron Ling Ching in "The Senator". The following notice was telegraphed after Mr. Crane's company appeared in Washington: "Dec 11, 1889 – The Chinaman entrusted to Mr. Braham was a decided success. His quaint philosophical resertations upon American customs and manners, uttered with the drollest voice, and with a countenance impressive as his mandarin prototype of the average tea chest, were always received with barrels of laughter and applause." Mr. Braham has circled the world five times and crossed the Atlantic twenty-three times. His home is America, he having bought property, in 1876, at Babylon L.I. His intention is to build a country home and reside there during the Summer.

There are a number of inconsistencies in the article, which could be attributed to artistic exaggeration. Regarding the shipwrecks: the *Queen of the Thames* was indeed wrecked on the Cape Coast on 17 March 1871. However it had set out from Plymouth to Melbourne on 20 November 1870 and was wrecked on its return voyage starting on 18 February. According to the notice in *The Era*, Harry was appearing at The Kensington Music Hall at New Year.

The *Rangoon* struck the Kadir rock and sank at Point of Galle Harbour, Ceylon (now Sri Lanka) on 1 November 1871. Harry was in Adelaide at the time.

Regarding the *Gutenberg* disaster – although there were a couple of ships of this name, there seems to be no trace of a mass loss of life in the Torres Strait apart from the *Quetta* with the loss of 200 on 28 February 1890, which was a couple of weeks after the article was written.

Harry was 20 when he visited Australia, not 15.

There seems to be no trace of the tour of China, Japan, India and Ceylon. His touring schedule of Australia, America and UK would not in any case have given him time to do these. Similarly, there is no trace of a tour of Aden, Suez, Jerusalem and the Pyramids – was this, perhaps, an illustration of the trip back through the Suez Canal on the steamship *Hankow* returning to London from Sydney?

There do not seem to be any newspaper articles about 'Pygmalion and his Galadear' touring Paris, Berlin and the European cities, merely his appearance in Paris, nor any articles concerning a trip to find gems at Kimberley, South Africa. Again, his touring schedule between 1871 and 1890 would have been unlikely to have enabled him to do this.

The most intriguing part of the article is the complete omission of Lizzie!

Crane took his plays on tour, but always came back to his 'resident' theatre, the Star in Brooklyn. This was the same theatre Harry had appeared in with Lizzie ten years previously. It must have brought back bittersweet memories.

In the midst of rehearsals and stage productions, Harry had not performed 'Masks and Faces' for three years, but he was asked to do so among many other different artistes for a special benefit for the child star Little Tuesday on 18 May 1890 – again, at the Star Theatre. Clearly he had not forgotten anything, for his act was loudly encored. Little Tuesday – her real name was Charlotte Selina Wood – was born in 1886 or 1887. A precocious child, by the time she was two she could sing, dance and act and she was put on the stage. Tuesday was the most well-known child star and a 'benefit' was held to provide education for her. Her career came to an abrupt end at the age of 7 when Eldridge T Gerry Jr, an Evangelical socialite and president of the Prevention of Cruelty to Children (also known at that time as The Gerry Society) helped bring in a ban on child performers under sixteen. Although this was met with hostile resistance by theatre managers – and some parents – it was eventually passed with some concessions for the theatrical world.

Harry had now settled into a routine: he would go home to see his family in June and return to New York in August to begin the next theatre season. The year drew to a close and he must have felt blessed. Maybe he was too complacent, because his life was about to change again.

CHAPTER THIRTEEN
Peril at Sea

Everyone on deck! All hands on deck! Fire! Fire! Bring the hose quick! As the steamship lurched in the heavy seas, Harry grabbed what clothes he could; coughing and with his eyes smarting from the smoke, he struggled with the other terrified passengers to climb the ladders. On deck, with the rain lashing down and the wind howling, he gripped the rails of the ship tightly, trying to stay upright. With horror he saw the flames leaping high in the hold and he thought his time had come.

Ironically, 1891 had started so well. In January, Harry's portrayal of Baron Ling Ching in 'The Senator' was being critically acclaimed and the play was still enjoying spectacular success. He was earning more money than in his days in Australia.

The following month, the stability of his life was shattered forever when, out of the blue, he received a telegram to say his father had died. Nathaniel had suffered from diabetes and circulation problems in his leg resulted in it becoming gangrenous: further fatal complications had set in.

From the beginning, Nathaniel's marriage to Susan had caused him great difficulties with his religious beliefs, and although he had married in an Anglican church, he had never renounced his Jewish faith. He was laid to rest by the family in the Western Synagogue Cemetery in Edmonton, London.

Harry was devastated and was now struggling with a moral dilemma. At the start of his career, relations between himself and his father had not always been good. This had changed with Harry's success and they had become fond of each other over the years, particularly when Nathaniel had come to see Harry in the USA and through his support in the difficult years afterwards. Harry dearly wished to go back to England to comfort his mother, but was contractually obliged to stay until the completion of the play's run at the end of May.

Harry contacted his mother, expressing his sorrow and saying that he was unable to break his contract but would take the next ship home at the end of the season. He forced himself to concentrate on the shows ahead, but the enthusiastic response of the crowd offered little consolation for the grief he felt inside.

Harry attended the traditional end-of-season banquet which was held by Crane for the whole company at the Clarendon Hotel in New York. For the first time though, he did not enjoy it – he was desperate to get home and see his family, but all the ships he had tried were full. It was the summer vacation and it seemed everyone was going to Europe.

After trudging for hours trying to find a berth on a ship, he finally managed to get a ticket on *The City of Richmond*, leaving on 6 June and bound for Liverpool. It was one of the faster steamships, also rigged for sail. Harry was glad to be able to get one of the first-class staterooms. With new electric light throughout the ship, plush saloon areas and modern bathrooms, it was like a hotel. It was a fine day when he boarded.

Harry was a seasoned traveller and had crossed the Atlantic by steamship over 20 times. He hadn't been on board an hour when he noticed there seemed to be an unusual amount of steam and a strange moth-eaten smell coming from below. Dismissing it as of no consequence, and as the crew did not seem concerned, he settled himself for the voyage.

The following day the conditions were so still that they made little headway, even with steam power. It was on 8 June that the weather turned, and an ordinary trip home unfolded into an unimaginable horror. It was windy at first, and then the rain started. Soon it was blowing a gale and the ship lurched as the seas became heavier. Many passengers were seasick. As the storm blew all that night, cases were tossed about and passengers tried to hold on to anything they could. Suddenly there was an almighty bang: it sounded like a collision and many started screaming.

The sound they heard was a massive wave crashing against the side of the ship. The storm continued raging all through the following day, but the stokers in their hot hell down below somehow managed to keep the steamer going.

The shout of fire came early on the morning of 10 June, waking everyone up with a heart-hammering start. That strange smell had become stronger. Harry started choking and could see smoke coming through the cabin door. Within minutes, all of the 200 passengers – from first-class, second-class and steerage – had climbed the ladders and were shivering on deck together. They then saw with horror the cause of the smoke: the crew had opened the hold and were fighting the fire which was raging amongst the 2,000 bales of cotton held there.

As the storm gathered pace the rain soaked Harry's clothes, and the salty water lashed the decks. Many people were still in their nightwear, clinging for dear life onto anything stable. A lot of the women were crying and praying fervently, the men comforting them while trying to contain their own emotions.

The crew tried valiantly to bring the blaze under control, but the storm had shown no sign of abating and it was proving difficult and hazardous. Somehow they managed to remove four smouldering bales, throwing them overboard. The Captain ordered the crew to close the hold and use the steam injectors to try and extinguish the rest of the flames, having already launched distress flares.

The crew had already started to prepare the lifeboats while Harry and the other male passengers tried to keep occupied by helping the cooks who were engaged in the seemingly futile task of providing enough food for everyone quickly, in case they had to abandon ship.

Out in the middle of the Atlantic, there seemed to be no hope of rescue, and Harry and his fellow passengers feared for their lives. Sleep was almost impossible, but they grabbed any rest they could in steamer chairs. The steerage passengers had moved into the saloon, sleeping where they could. Harry's clothes were now torn and grimy, and even if he could have got to his luggage there seemed no point in changing, as it seemed they would surely burn or sink to the bottom of the ocean.

On the morning of 11 June, a ship came into sight. The passengers had seen its lights in the distance, but either it hadn't seen them or it had ignored the distress flares. They were despairing when suddenly the ship came back into view – it was coming towards them! The ship's name was the *Counsellor*. Its Captain, John G Jones, had originally thought that the flares were early Independence Day rockets, but when he realised the *Richmond* was in trouble, he sailed back to help them. Harry and the rest of the passengers let out a loud cheer of relief.

With the storm still raging, Captain Redford had already concluded that it would be useless to launch the *Richmond*'s lifeboats – although the deck was still hot, at least the fire seemed to have been put out. In the midst of the drama and the realisation that rescue was now a real possibility, Captain Redford was horrified when – as he was exchanging signals with the *Counsellor* – Captain Jones suddenly collapsed.

As the officers and crew rushed to the Captain's assistance, it soon became apparent he was dead – they could do nothing but take his body below. The *Counsellor*'s Chief Officer William Darton quickly took over from Captain Jones and signalled to the *Richmond* that they would stay alongside in case any assistance was required.

The passengers' initial relief at imminent rescue later turned to panic when a rumour went round that the *Counsellor*'s Captain had died of yellow fever. To make matters worse, they discovered that there were 140 barrels of paraffin oil stored near the smouldering cotton: the heat coming from the hold did not appear to have cooled and even the pitch was melting.

Throughout this time Captain Redford's manner had calmed many of the passengers and he had kept them up-to-date with developments. He reassured them that the oil was far enough away not to be a hazard, that the fire had been contained and that Jones' sudden death had not been due to fever.

Harry then saw another two other, larger ships heading towards them – the *City of Paris* and the *Servia*, both faster ships than the *Counsellor*.

Once alongside the stricken ship, Captain Redford, Officer Darton and the *Servia*'s Captain decided that as the *Servia* and *Richmond* sailed at the same speed it would be better for the *Counsellor* and the *City of Paris* to continue on their own routes.

As they neared England the weather calmed down, and early on 15 June Harry at last saw the lights of Liverpool as the city was waking up. He was exhausted but he was still alive! He was only 40 but felt he had aged considerably in the last few days. Dirty, dishevelled and unshaven, he was one of the first passengers off the ship when the ship finally docked at about 8am. His luggage was ruined, but relief was written all over his face as he gave a graphic description of the drama to a waiting reporter from the *New York Herald* who said, as the passengers disembarked, that he "never saw human beings happier to reach firm land." Harry said:

> Don't say a word, dear boy; haven't had my clothes off in five days. Thought it unnecessary to make any changes as I believed we were going to be buried or drowned, never was so glad in my life to see the shore – even a foreign shore. Closest thing I ever experienced though I've crossed about twenty five times; life on a burning steamer is completely lacking in humor, it is no fun to wake up in the middle of the night and hear the sailors yell "More water!" or to get up in the morning for the sole purpose of trying whether the deck is hotter or cooler than the night before.
>
> I sailed on the Richmond because there was no other boat. Hadn't been on board an hour when I noticed an unusual quantity of steam from the cylinders. The same night the ship stopped six hours to pack the cylinders. Down below there was the most unpleasant moth-eaten smell I noticed the water coming through the ports when they were closed ... The bad weather began on the 8th; a terrible sea struck the ship on the morning of the 9th and the ship shivered so all thought that a collision had occurred. The next morning a lady felt the deck near the cabin hot and saw smoke coming through she called the steward, but he paid no attention to the smoke, but went on with his usual work.
>
> On the morning of the 10th I saw smoke coming out of the fore hold. I was nearly asphyxiated in my cabin, I heard an officer shout "for God's sake bring a hose

quick!" when the fore hold was opened I saw the blaze plainly. The passengers were thrown into a panic, orders were given to provision the boats, there was a terrible sea and Captain Redford afterward said not one of the boats could have lived to get twelve yards from the ship. The women stood it well. The Captain, officers and crew worked like Trojans. We gave the Captain and officers a testimonial and the crew £80.00.

The decks were so hot the pitch melted, and you could dry wet boots in a few minutes. The Servia's passengers said they could see the steam rise when the sea washed the plates above the water line. On the 11th the captain said it was an even thing whether he could keep the fire under. The same day we heard there was a lot of petroleum on board. This was great consolation. The cotton in which the fire broke out was not fresh and was therefore highly inflammable.

The crew showed the greatest bravery in fighting the fire. The ship is in a sense sea-worthy, but is unfit for first class passengers. Five days of fire, with death staring us in the face added at least a year to my age. Everybody's luggage was more or less damaged; but we are all so glad to reach land.

The euphoria of landing safely was quick to disappear as he boarded the train to London, in the knowledge that this time he would not see his father. His mother had moved to a smaller house in St Pancras High Street with Edwin and a servant. When he was greeted by them, his delight at being reunited with his mother at last was tempered by the sight of her still in mourning clothes. His loss became reality, and the family grieved together for the first time.

Harry had only been back in England for a few weeks when, all too soon, he realised he would have to go back across the Atlantic to join the company for another season. He had travelled the world and had been incredibly lucky to have only been involved in one minor ship accident back in 1874: this new near-disaster, though, had really traumatised him. It would not be easy to sail again, but he had no option.

The steamer *The City of Paris*, which had nearly come to his rescue, was leaving from Liverpool for New York on 5 August. What better ship to sail on, to regain his confidence in travelling? Even though it was a luxurious ship with walnut panelling, hot and cold running water and electric ventilation, he still embarked with trepidation, alert to every sound and smell. Fortunately, this time the trip passed uneventfully. He re-joined Crane and the company to rehearse 'The Senator' again for the play's opening in Providence, Rhode Island, on 14 September. What a reunion it would be – and what a tale he had to tell!

CHAPTER FOURTEEN
Breaking Away

When Harry returned to the Star Theatre in New York, in January 1892, it had recently undergone redecoration with plush curtains in the vestibule and stained-glass signage brilliantly illuminated with electric light, with Crane's name and the play's title in large letters. The drama of the previous year faded away, and rehearsals began in earnest for Crane's new play 'For Money'. Crane again played the lead, this time as a man who had never fired a gun but was a colonel of a regiment – and who was a commodore of a yachting club but scared of the water!

Star Theatre, New York, 1900

The play revolved around the romance of his daughter, and sorting out fortune-hunters from friends. Harry played the character of Parker, the butler, and his performance gained good reviews. Crane was keen to put on another play before the end of the season, but 'For Money' was so successful he nearly had to abandon the idea.

103

However, in April Harry appeared as the black servant Drinkwater in the next play, 'The American Minister'.

This was a four-act play set in Rome about a State Department minister, played by Crane, arriving to find an important despatch had been stolen and his son accused of the theft, when in reality it had been stolen by the mafia, threatening world peace. He then recovered the document through various sub-plots, clearing his son's name and averting disaster.

With the season finished, Harry made preparations for his usual vacation in England. It was the first time he had sailed back home since his near-fatal journey the year before: there was no other method of travel, and any fears he may have had just had to be overcome.

He spent the time in England catching up with friends and family, and attending plays until it was time to head back to the USA. For years he had arrived at the main immigration point of Castle Garden, but this had become too cramped for the number of people arriving and was unwelcoming too, with hawkers and low boarding houses outside. Now he was to go to a new building on Ellis Island which had opened just a few months previously: at three storeys tall and made of Georgia pine, it was bright, spacious and had all the facilities any visitor could want. It must have been a refreshing change.

Crane had decided to begin the season again with another run of 'The Senator', but needed to employ another leading lady to take over the part vacated by Georgie Drew Barrymore who had to retire due to ill health. He decided to engage another well-known actress – Agnes Booth, an Australian. Her fame was not restricted to her acting, but also had come about through her marriage to Junius Brutus Booth Jr – the brother of John Wilkes Booth who had assassinated President Abraham Lincoln. The company was in such close contact with each other for weeks, staying at the same hotel wherever they went, that her connection to her infamous brother-in-law was probably brought up in more than one conversation.

'The Senator' began again in 1893 and, as before, gained rave reviews: it toured widely through Wisconsin and Michigan, with the company travelling by special trains. Most of the theatrical season was taken up with it, and by the time the company finished at the Star in New York, they were exhausted. When Harry returned to the UK that summer he had decided that, although he was enjoying the celebrity and money, he was starting to get bored with the play and vowed to leave the company the following year.

Harry attended the lavish New Year's Eve supper, which Crane had again organised for his artistes. The theatre was bedecked in flowers and decorations, and the invitations were gold-embossed. As Harry looked around and chatted to his friends and fellow actors, he probably pondered whether he had made the right decision. Acting and singing could be a precarious business. Just days after that party, on the other side of the world, Richard Ramsden died an alcoholic at the age of 60: when his voice went, his singing career was finished and he had been scratching a living copying music and serving as a doorman at various theatres before dying from a fall at his Melbourne lodging house.

Sheet-music from The Senator

In January it was back to playing in 'The Senator' once more, and Harry asked Crane if he could be released from his contract at the end of the season as he wanted to try new things. Although Crane was surprised, he realised that after five years of mostly playing the same character parts as a low comedian, Harry probably needed a fresh challenge. He agreed, wishing him well for the future.

At liberty for the first time, Harry felt a burden had been lifted and left as usual for the UK in June 1894. Wanting to try out his solo work again, an opportunity presented itself when he heard about a performance at the Pavilion in London to celebrate the 35th anniversary of the theatre. He offered his services and was glad to be given a spot on the bill: a review a couple of days later, mentioning his artistic song with apt facial expressions, was very favourable. He had obviously lost none of his old magic and it felt good to be doing his own act again after so long.

When he returned to the USA in September, to his home in West 34th Street, Harry placed an advertisement in the *New York Dramatic Mirror*, one of the main dramatic trade papers, announcing that he was available for engagements. He was surprised but delighted when, shortly afterwards, he was offered an opportunity of headlining in a play written specially for him as Solomon, in 'Moses and Son', acting in blackface.

Most theatrical managers were based on Broadway and Kaufmann's office was at number 180. Meeting him there, Harry discussed the project and Kaufmann booked the tour – but Harry was given the freedom to get his own company together, including the costumes and scenery (which he naturally had to pay for himself). It opened, to Harry's great excitement, on 19 November 1894 in Bridgeport, Connecticut.

At first all seemed well and he was getting good attendances, but it soon became apparent the play was a commercial failure and it closed in mid-December. This was a bitter blow and, embarrassed after the success he had had, he wasted no time in sailing for Europe in January 1895 to find work in a more fruitful venture. He did not return to the USA for nearly five years.

After some time catching up with his family, he went to Hamburg in early March to appear in 'Morocco Bound', a two-act farcical play by Arthur Branscombe. He played the lead of Spoofah Bey, an Irish con man who was getting a variety of characters to play the stars of the music hall, enabling him to gain a theatrical contract. He then appeared at the Unter Den Linden theatre in Berlin later that month. This time the play was a success, and his old optimism came back. His delight did not last long, however: his mother Susan had been feeling unwell for some time and after tests it was discovered she had cancer.

Harry returned to England in June, going to her new address in Finborough Road, Kensington, where she was staying with Edwin. Harry was distraught and hoped for a miracle but it was not to be and she died three months later on 5 September.

Although his relationship with his father had sometimes been testing, Harry was very close to his mother and he was heartbroken, placing advertisements in the UK, USA and Australian papers about his loss. The week after her funeral he still had an engagement to fill – after this he did not appear on stage for nearly a year. It had been his mother's last wish that Edwin should be looked after and after discussions an aunt agreed that he should live with her in Uverdale Road, Chelsea. Harry also moved in while he decided what to do next.

1896 was a rough year: Harry had no wish to work, and indeed had only done his solo act a couple of times. He had also been away from the UK for a number of years and for the first time began having money problems, having also lost money from the failed play. He entrusted a number of engravings and documents to a Mr J A Lewis of Brompton Fine Art Gallery in November 1896 for him to sell on commission, but in April when he had not received them back, he took Lewis to court.

One of the prints was of John Wilkes Booth, with his autograph. Lewis stated it was a copy and not worth anything and anyway, he had mislaid the property. As Harry had worked with Booth's sister-in-law, it is highly likely that it was original: the case was found for Harry and Lewis was ordered to give them up.

By the end of 1896, Harry had recovered sufficiently and managed to obtain work. He was acting at the Eden Theatre in Brighton in the pantomime 'Dick Whittington' as Alderman Fitzwarren. When the pantomime finished in January 1897, he was presented with a fine umbrella.

He then began doing his solo performances again; he was thrilled to find they were still popular after doing them for 20 years, and he started getting regular all-year-round work. In 1898, Harry was still touring with 'Masks and Faces' before going back to the legitimate stage in the play 'The War Correspondent' at the Princes Theatre in Portsmouth in December.

Between engagements, he went back home to Chelsea. He found out that Edwin had not paid a tailor's bill and had been taken to court. Harry had another commitment to fulfil, so Charles went to act as defence witness. Laughter ensued in court when Edwin confused his occupation of betting clerk or 'turf accountant' with being an accountant. Over the next few years, Edwin's mental health deteriorated and caused much worry: they had always been a close family and instead of being sent to an institution, he was cared for at home by his brother Charles and his nieces.

Another busy year was ahead: in 1899 Harry crossed the Atlantic a number of times. Always generous-hearted, like most music-hall artistes when benefits were needed, he appeared in February in San Francisco for a benefit to open a reform home for boys and in April for comic vocalist Max Steinle. Immediately after this, he returned to the UK as he was engaged to perform on the same bill at the Crystal Palace with La Loie Fuller, who had become famous for her serpentine dance at the Folies Bergère in Paris. La Loie Fuller, who was born Marie Louise Fuller in Chicago in 1862, was a pioneer of both modern dancing and theatrical lighting techniques, using silk costumes in a free natural movement, illuminated by lighting of her own design using chemical salts and colour gels which she patented. Although known more as an actress in America, having started her career as a child, she had choreographed dances for burlesque and circus but she felt she was not taken seriously as a dancer – so she transferred to Paris after a European tour, where her techniques had been warmly applauded. She became popular with Henri de Tolouse Lautrec and Marie Curie, and became the embodiment of the Art Nouveau movement.

After his Crystal Palace show, Harry then continued touring with his solo act before sailing for France, to open at the 1900 Paris exposition in Charles McCarthy's play 'A Great New York Fire'. New productions were always a financial risk with any manager and McCarthy later went bankrupt, owing Harry $2,000.

CHAPTER FIFTEEN
Citizen Braham

Harry returned to New York in 1900 and rented an apartment on West 45th Street: he had always loved America ever since he had toured there in the 1870s and now – with the loss of his parents – he was convinced he should be based there, particularly as he was able to obtain more work in the USA than in his native country. He acquired American citizenship on 8 March 1900, joining immigrants arriving from all over the world.

In November he returned to San Francisco: the city was now a hectic mix of the new invention of the motorcar, trolleys, horse and carriages, and pedestrians. With no traffic control, it was hazardous just trying to get to his next performances at the Alcazar Theatre to appear in 'His Absent Boy'. From there, he transferred to Chutes Theatre in his own act, and then on to Fischers Concert Hall in January 1901.

In April he again met up with La Loie Fuller and her company to appear in 'An Accidental Sweetheart' in Salem, Oregon and again in May at the Margaret Theatre in Anaconda, Montana. The *Anaconda Standard* loved his performance:

> Harry Braham is well known and admired in many parts of the world and American and English papers are loud in their praise of him. His portrayals of Minister Wu, Kaiser Wilhelm, President MacKinley [sic], Oom Paul Kruger – State President of the South African Republic – (Transvaal), George Washington and an old maid, and a series of facial expressions were remarkable.

In January 1902, he was again playing in 'Morocco Bound' at the Columbia Theatre in Boston: the play ran for three months before going on tour to Portsmouth, New Hampshire and Fitchburg, Massachusetts. By the end of the year, Harry wanted to travel outside the USA again and found out that the English Dramatic and

*Harry as Picorin the Baker
Sergeant Kitty, 1904*

Comedy Concert Party were going to Jamaica in January 1903 and needed a comedian. He applied and they were delighted to employ him – he was well known and would attract audiences.

Harry was the headline act when the company opened at the Theatre Royal in Kingston, Jamaica, on 3 February. Harry wondered if he should have agreed to go when a minor earthquake shook the western half of the island. Two weeks later they played in Spanish Town, Montego Bay, Port Maria and Annotto Bay before returning to Kingston. The company later moved on but Harry loved the island and stayed to appear in various towns in his solo act throughout Jamaica, not returning to the USA until July – and just missing the massive Hurricane Gilbert which devastated the island a month later.

New York had changed a lot in the two years since he had been away. The old Star Theatre, where he had appeared so many times, was now demolished; the massive new Flatiron building looked strange by itself and towered over everything; even taller buildings were being designed and built; and he arrived to another new immigration station on Ellis Island – this time made of brick to replace the wooden building, which had burnt down in 1897. If he felt a touch of sadness when he saw where the Star once stood, he did not have much time for reflection as it was not long before he was back working. He was cast in George R White's production of the comic opera 'Sergeant Kitty' as Picorin the Baker, the main star being Virginia Earle, a leading lady of light operetta (reviews in the early 1900s stated that she was without a rival in her field). They opened at the Montauk Theatre in Brooklyn in November.

A lot of theatres were now lit by electricity, which should have made them safer than the previous gas systems, yet fire regulations were still primitive and were often overlooked in favour of profit. This was tragically proved all too true when the largest loss of life in theatre occurred in Chicago, when the newly built Iroquois Theatre caught fire due to an electrical shortage on 30 December 1903. Exits were barred and obscured by curtains and a new type of lock had been fitted which many people were unfamiliar with. In the resulting stampede over 600 died, many of them women and children.

Newspapers carried reports of the full horror of the fire, and caused an outrage when it was revealed that the deficiencies had been covered up by the owners. As a result, New York theatres started banning standing room, and all over the country building exits were configured so that they were clearly marked and could be opened from the inside.

'Sergeant Kitty' transferred to Broadway and then went on tour. White, however, had financial problems and though the play and its company were a great success and had been supposed to transfer to the UK and Australia the following year, White went bankrupt. He owed the cast and stage-hands many thousands of dollars: Harry lost £250 – a not inconsiderable sum. Experience over the years had taught him that whenever he was engaged in a play, the risks were not only that the play itself might fail, but that the manager might fail too. Although it was a blow, it was not altogether a surprise.

In January 1906 Harry was engaged to appear at the Eden Musee in New York on 23rd Street in 'Masks and Faces'. The audiences flocked to the unusual entertainment complex, which was a flamboyant mix of ornate architecture and statues, with five entrances – it was the first venue in the city to show motion pictures. Also on offer for their amusement were waxworks of royal figures and presidents, and a chamber of horrors. They could marvel at the feats of jugglers and acrobats, listen to singers and an orchestra in the winter garden, or take refreshments in the café and have a game of chess with Ajeeb, the 10-foot robot (in reality a papier mâché figure operated by its maker inside).

Harry was praised in the magazine *Variety* for his "clever and unique act", his engagement lasting till the middle of April.

He enjoyed going to see various other artistes and plays when he had some rare leisure time in between rehearsals and shows. At this time Harry Houdini was appearing at the Vaudeville Theatre and it is possible that he would have seen Houdini's act. Houdini had just returned from Europe where, in a spectacular demonstration, he had broken out of 63 prison cells: he then issued a challenge to the New York police to choose their best handcuffs and manacles and bring them to the Union Square Theatre to test him. He had also had police from different states trying to devise handcuffs to hold him – their efforts were in vain, leading him to be called 'The King of Handcuffs'.

1907 was a very busy year: Harry went on a 10-month tour of the western states – including appearances in Winnipeg; Des Moines, Iowa; Fort Wayne, Indiana; and Duluth, Montana – in his solo show 'Harry Braham – The Man with One Hundred Faces and Characters from Charles Dickens'. He commissioned a publicity poster showcasing the acts he had done on the stage and in his show 'Masks and Faces': the picture took up the whole of the front page of the *New York Dramatic Mirror* on the same day of his appearance in Winnipeg on 13 April.

Harry on tour in 1907

On 10 August Harry returned to a very different San Francisco to appear at the newly built Orpheum Theatre. Just over a year earlier, while he had been at the Eden Musee, San Francisco had been hit by a massive earthquake which, along with the fire that followed, had destroyed over 80 percent of the buildings. Thousands had been killed and most of the theatres Harry had appeared in the 1870s had been razed to the ground. The city, though, had fought back and was rebuilding: it was a testament to the San Francisco people and of how important entertainment was to them, that the theatre on Ellis St was opened in January, a mere nine months later.

This tour was when he brought his knowledge of Dickens into his performances: Dickens' lectures were more like storytelling and Dickens' account of the death of Nancy in *Oliver Twist* was said to have taken so much out of him that it made him ill. As Harry's was

113

Advertisement for Harry's Mask and Faces tour, 1907

an individual act, and he was continually travelling, it was important that he did not need too many changes of costume and this is where his unique act came into its own – he could convey so many different characters purely by a change of expression. In the show, he conveyed the characters of Dickens' most popular characters, including Micawber, Scrooge, and Fagin, to wide acclaim.

Little is known about what Harry did after his solo tour: a report in a newspaper of August 1910 talks about him having returned to America after touring the world. What we do know is that Harry appeared in December 1910 at the Hyperion Theatre in New Haven, in an English social comedy by William L Branscombe called 'We Can't be as Bad as All That' which transferred to New York in January 1911. He then appeared as Stuff in the morality play 'Everywoman' by Walter Browne. A newspaper article appeared in the Brooklyn newspaper, the *Daily Standard Union* on 18 June giving a glowing report of his abilities:

> Harry Braham the protean actor-vocalist, who has gained distinction in Europe and America for his humorous "Masks and Faces" has been engaged by Henry W. Savage for the part of Stuff in the special "Everywoman" company which will open in Chicago in September. Mr Braham was long ago recognised as a clever actor.

In 1911, Harry Rickards died and Harry Braham wrote an obituary for the New York Clipper. Although Harry had known Rickards well, the article is very detached and Lizzie is mentioned only as Rickard's co-star. He mentions the 'disagreement' which led to Rickards and Lizzie parting to form their own companies. What he doesn't say is that Lizzie was his wife and the 'disagreement' occurred because of Lizzie's wish to part from his company and to start a new one with Harry. In the obituary he describes Rickards as 'the Napoleon of the Antipodes'.

> Harry Rickards, Australian vaudeville manager and London comic singer, who died in London, Eng., recently, was born in that country in 1841. His father was an engine driver, and Harry was articled to his father's trade and served his time at Nine Elms, London

Southwestern Engineer Shops. While there Harry had the top of his fingers cut off by a machine lathe, but fortunately the machine cut through the flesh of the fingers and escaped the bone.

Very early in life he gave up the locomotive, and took to the music hall, then an institution supervised by a chairman who announced the artists before they appeared, and naturally led the applause with his hammer. Harry, being a good looking young fellow, soon made his mark as a vocal comedian. His first big hit was "Captain Jinks of the Horse Marines," afterwards made famous in America by William Horace Lingard. This was followed by other popular hits.

After touring Great Britain and the London halls, his salary was about twenty pounds in the provinces per week, and for the London halls about six pounds a turn. Then he made a contract with Enderby Jackson, of Hull, to visit the Australian colonies, and with his co-star, Lizzie Watson, set sail from London in a clipper sailing ship in 1871, arriving in Melbourne, Australia, at the end of the same year. He opened up at the St. George's Hall, in the above named city, to big business, giving the entire show with Miss Watson. He was styled the greatest comic singer in the world, and Miss Watson was called Great Britain's star serio comic singer. After finishing Melbourne, they went to Sydney and played a season at the School of Arts. Then they disagreed, and Rickards and Watson started out on tour with their separate companies.

Mr. Rickards eventually made his way to 'Frisco, and played a short engagement for the late Tom Maguire. This was about 1875. He played the continent and reached New York, where he played for Josh Hart at the old Theatre Comique, Broadway, below Niblo's Garden. Later he returned to London and the British provinces and then he returned to the Antipodes, this time to locate there.

After a very successful tour he began his managerial

career in Sydney, at the old Scandinavian Music Hall, an old disused music hall on Castlereagh Street, and turned it into a most profitable resort, calling it the Tivoli. Then he branched out in Melbourne, Adelaide, Brisbane, and engaged the highest priced talent from America, England and the continent of Europe, and at the time of his death was very wealthy, leaving an estate worth upwards of four hundred thousand pounds. He leaves a wife, a professional, and two daughters, one of whom is in the profession. Mr. Rickards' name in private life was Benjamin Leete. His brothers will look after all his Australian theatrical interests.

HARRY N. BRAHAM

In 1912, when the whole world was shocked at the disaster of the sinking of the *Titanic*, Harry had his own tragedy to deal with: Edwin was seriously ill and had been taken to hospital. Having suffered for so long, Edwin died on 24 June from vascular dementia. He was only 58.

Edwin Braham

CHAPTER SIXTEEN
Moving Pictures

Always versatile, Harry kept changing with the times: he had come from the early minstrel years to music hall and the 'legitimate' stage. Now a new technology had come along – moving pictures.

Harry had been fascinated by the invention of the cinematograph since its beginnings in the late 1890s. He had watched the progression of film making and its increasing sophistication. In an article for the *New York Clipper* (17 February 1912), he said:

> The American and English speaking people want natural gesticulation, and the art of acting is to be natural, so to-day we are getting clean comedy and drama. The slap-stick and the monkey antics of the last decade are fast disappearing, and instead of the foreign film being in demand it is the American article that is in use in every country under the sun.
>
> The time is not far distant when stars of the first magnitude will pose and star in parts made popular by them, and why not? No actor, be he great or small, should look down on the film actor. There are hundreds of idle Thespians only too glad to get that five dollar bill daily, especially in these days when theatrical engagements are so difficult to obtain. Most of the big companies have their stock company, consisting of twenty or more capable people, who receive good salaries for fifty-two weeks in the year. These companies have several stage directors, many of whom are capable of staging the elaborate productions seen on the stages of the Broadway theatres. These gentlemen not only tell and show the actor stage business, but they also teach them how to utilize their facial muscles.

From his perspective, he thought film actors had an easy life, with everything laid on – from make-up artists to costumiers and food provision. They did not have to tread the boards 'burning the midnight oil' as he had done, gaining experience through hard work and much financial hardship.

He had acted in all areas of theatre: now he wanted to experience film for himself. He got his chance to do this in *Suppressed Evidence*, a short which was released by the Kalem Company in May 1912, just a month before Edwin died.

The method by which actors prepared for a film was very different to preparing for the stage. In an article for the *New York Dramatic Mirror* Harry said:

> The difference between the regular stage and the moving picture rehearsal, is that the stage-manager or author of the legitimate, reads his play to the company, after which the parts are handed out and a rehearsal takes place. Business of the piece is written in. This goes on until the actors are conversant with their lines, then parts are discarded, and the real acting takes place; for it is impossible to feel a part until such time that one is dead-letter perfect. The moving picture rehearsals are vastly different. The director calls his company around him, and with scenario in hand calls the ladies and gentlemen by their names, first mentioning what the wordless play is. "Mr. ___ you are a lover. Miss ___ you are his affianced bride. Mrs. ___ you are the mother. Mr. ___ you are the father. Mr. ___ you are the villain" and so on. Thus the different scenes are rehearsed without parts, the director explaining the business and, as the playlet proceeds, he elaborates and builds up situations and sensations that the author never dreamed of.

In June Harry's second film was released – *Vengeance of Heaven*, a Mutual production. He then went back to California to make two more films scheduled to be shown in 1915 – *The Fight* and then probably the most controversial epic ever made – *Birth Of A Nation* directed by D W Griffith.

The film, based on the book and play *The Clansman* by Thomas Dixon Jr, was filmed in 1914 and released on 8 February 1915: it was the first 'blockbuster', running for 3 hours 10 minutes, and grossing $10 million in its initial release, creating a box-office record that would not be shattered until *Gone With The Wind* in 1939. Incorporating many breakthroughs in film technique, it pioneered panoramic long shots, night photography, iris effects, panning camera, and battle scenes using hundreds of extras – making them look like thousands. It was the first film to be shown at The White House, seen by the then President Woodrow Wilson.

The subject-matter of the film concerned the star-crossed lovers of two families, the Northern Stonemans and the Southern Camerons, in pre-Civil War America. The families are friends, but the Civil War puts them on opposite sides – Elsie Stoneman (played by Lillian Gish) and Ben Cameron fall in love; as do Phil Stoneman and Margaret Cameron. The film featured Afro-Americans played by white men in blackface and portrayed black men as being unintelligent and aggressive towards white women: the Ku Klux Klan were portrayed as heroes. On the film's release, it caused an outcry against racism and the film was banned in several cities. It has remained an important and influential film, however, studied by universities and colleges for its depictions of attitudes to slavery and racism, and for its pioneering film techniques. It was also notable for Lillian Gish's performance as Elsie Stoneman: one of the first real 'stars' of the silent screen, Gish was to have a career spanning 75 years – her last appearance was in 1987 when, at the age of 93, she played opposite Bette Davis and Vincent Price in *The Whales of August*.

Although Harry was uncredited, he played Cameron's faithful black servant: for this role he went back to the very start of his career when he appeared in blackface. He was in a number of scenes: in the first half he can be clearly seen being flogged against a tree, being released and returning to his 'master' to help rescue him, after Dr Cameron was arrested for having a Klan costume (property of his son, Ben), which was a crime punishable by death. He also appeared in the second half, towards the end of the film, defending his 'master' to the death after being cornered in a hut by a brigade of Union 'freed slaves'.

Harry in blackface in DW Griffith's Birth of a Nation, 1915

Although there is no record of what Harry thought of D W Griffith as a director, he was an admirer of the art of film direction, as he commented in his article for the *New York Dramatic Mirror*:

> It is really surprising how the director, with the eyes of an eagle, sees instantly any defects in posing or grouping; for to keep a large number of people in action, as well as the principal characters (who depict in dumb show the story of the scenario) is no easy matter. The director, with a megaphone, calls the actors by their names, tells them the business of the piece, and what to do in facial expressions. "Miss So and So, do this! Smile! Open your eyes!" "Mr. So and So, your beard is not straight!" So you can see that the director's position is anything but an easy one. And the great secret of a director's success is to keep his temper.

Harry was still returning occasionally to London to see his brother Charles and his family. When he finished the film, he sailed back to the UK with the exciting news of his appearance in it. Though the family were familiar with Harry's work on stage, he had not played over in Britain for many years. He also wanted his favourite nephew, Cecil, to return to the USA with him, regaling him with stories of the film industry and how he was certain it would make a lot of money and turn actors into the stars of the future. The family, however, refused to believe he had been in such a famous film, and Cecil refused to go with him. Furious – and after a heated row – Harry called Cecil a "goddamn fool", slammed the door and was gone. Cecil was to become a rag-and-bone man.

CHAPTER SEVENTEEN
The Final Curtain

After so many years of touring, Harry's health was now starting to fail, and he had developed a chronic kidney condition. The pull of the stage was still strong and he travelled to Toronto in September 1916, appearing in the production of 'Silent Sue', before going back to New York in January for 'Boys will be Boys'. It was becoming clear, however, that he could not continue working at the same pace, but he figured that if he had to stop working or die, then he might as well be in a hit show. So he signed up to play in an operetta, 'Miss Springtime', which was getting rave reviews. Produced by Klaw and Erlanger, it boasted P G Wodehouse as its co-lyricist. Harry was given the part of Hugo Knau. He went with the company to Wisconsin before the play transferred to Oakland, California in December 1917 where his performance was acclaimed in the press. This show did indeed prove to be Harry's last professional engagement. No longer able to work and with no health service available, any savings he had made began to run out. He had made a lot of money in the past but by 1921, at the age of 70, he was destitute. Most of his friends were dead and after a bitter dispute he was no longer in contact with the family.

All entertainers knew of the Actors Fund. He desperately needed a place to stay where he could be cared for in his twilight years, though whether Harry approached the Fund or others did so on his behalf is not known. Fortunately there was an Actors Fund Home near West Brighton on Staten Island, set up especially for that purpose for those in the theatrical profession.

The only rules for admittance to the Home were sponsorship from two people confirming that the person was a respectable citizen with no other means of support who had given good service in their field, and not suffering from alcoholism or a terminal illness. Harry qualified but spaces were limited: his old manager W H Crane was on the board of directors of The Actors Fund and this probably helped him secure a room.

Actors Fund Home, West Brighton, Staten Island

As Harry was taken on the ferry, he could see Manhattan, Ellis Island and the Statue of Liberty fading into the distance behind him. A car was there to meet and transfer him the three miles down a country road to the home. When the car turned through the gates he could see this was no ordinary retirement home – it was a magnificent three-storey Elizabethan-style mansion set in 14 acres by a peaceful lake surrounded by woods. As he entered the hallway there was a huge open fireplace with comfortable leather chairs in cosy corners; going through the house he could see no expense had been spared – there was a billiard room, sewing room, smoking room, library, and a parlour with card tables. There was a magnificent dining room with windows opening onto a piazza where he would take his meals with the other residents. Out in the garden there were chairs to while away the summer days. The whole house was furnished by the most famous department store in New York – Macy's, with the best decorations available. He even had his own room, which would be decorated to his own taste. He found he was called a 'guest', not a resident. He could come and go as he pleased, just letting the superintendent of the home know where he was going. There were about 40 other guests who came from all areas of entertainment and enough staff to cater for their every need. The atmosphere inside was like a luxurious theatrical boarding house, but where no alcohol was allowed.

The guests were taken on outings and if they required anything, they just requested it. There were still opportunities for the old thespians to relive the old days when those who were able to could perform at 'Old Timer's Night', a vaudeville benefit show at the Palace Theatre in the neighbouring town of Port Richmond.

On Sunday evenings, entertainments were given in the drawing room. Christmas was also made a special time when a magnificent dinner was cooked and younger actors came and entertained them from the mainland, bringing presents.

After a lifetime of travelling, it was time for a rest.

As Harry sat in his chair in this beautiful house looking out at the lake, he probably thought back upon his life, his early days with the smells and dirt of London, the excitement of the minstrels and performing for the Queen, the journey with Tommy to the other side of the world in the clipper, and the euphoria as success followed success. Then there was Lizzie – the love, applause and heartbreak. So many theatres and plays – 'The Senator' was definitely the best. No one had surpassed his performance of Ling Ching which was still talked about all these years later. Where had the time gone? It seemed like only yesterday.

The *City of Richmond* fire – now that was scary! He could still remember the choking smoke. He had been so lucky to survive and had gone on to do so many other things, but he was tired now and he knew his time was running out. He would never again hear the applause on stage, or act in any more films. He foresaw how popular they would be – right from their beginning in the 1890s. He had been in the most famous film in the world and the family hadn't believed him. Now it was too late and they were lost to him.

By 1923, two years after he came to live in the home, Harry's kidney condition had worsened. In August he started getting pains in his chest and had trouble breathing; a doctor was called to the home and diagnosed heart inflammation. Harry was taken to Staten Island hospital where he passed away suddenly on 21 September, eight days after his 73rd birthday.

The Actors Fund paid for Harry's funeral, which took place at The Frank Campbell Funeral Church on Broadway, New York where the services of many famous actors and actresses including that of Rudolph Valentino were held. He was cremated and his ashes interred in the Actors Fund plot at Evergreen Cemetery in Brooklyn, New York.

AFTERWORD

Harry's working life spanned the whole of the period from minstrelsy to music hall, from theatre to silent film: it is an era that is now mostly forgotten, but which is vital for understanding how modern-day entertainment evolved.

His story is of a man born into poverty who travelled the world – bringing theatre, music and laughter to millions prior to the advent of modern travel and ease of communication. He also represents the thousands of lesser-known music-hall performers who paved the way for the more famous stars of the time, such as Marie Lloyd, Dan Leno and Little Tich – and for the film stars of the future.

The rich resources of the internet meant that I could research Harry's life through the many newspaper articles written about him. I had not known of his incredible career and adventures until a chance conversation with a friend in the Britannia, one of the many music halls he appeared in over 100 years ago – and one of the very few left. The newspaper articles about his performances, however, can never really give an insight into what he was like as a person: I have only fleeting anecdotes from family members, such as their tales of the final row within the family. For his early life in particular, any feelings that Harry and his parents had can only be surmised and I have had to use the evidence of census, certificates and newspaper reports about Nathaniel together with historical information about the conditions of the time.

During my research I came up against a difficulty which caused all sorts of confusion, and that was the 'other' Harry Braham, who was born in 1855 in London and died in 1938 in the USA. Harry was a composer, and when he married the American beauty Lillian Russell in 1879 the papers naturally took note, for Lillian was the greatest actress/singer of that period, and her private life was as flamboyant as her acting career.

Lillian had already been married when she fell in love and they had a child, also named Harry, who died as a baby after his nurse accidentally stuck him with a nappy pin. In 1885, Lillian divorced Harry and married another composer, Edward Solomon. However, Mr Solomon was still married to a serio-comic named Lily Grey in England and he was arrested for bigamy.

'Harry's Boys', circa 1901

A curious co-incidence occurred, in that 'our' Harry appeared a number of times with Lily Grey, and he would have undoubtedly been aware of the circumstances surrounding Edward Solomon and Lillian. He may have talked to Lily about it and maybe even about his own similar circumstances with Lizzie. It was also confusing because Tony Pastor was involved in the careers of Lillian and both Harry Brahams!

Because Lillian Russell was one of the most talked-about women and whose name and likeness adorned many papers, whenever I searched for Harry's name during my research, I often found that I was reading about the 'other' Harry! Thankfully, although both were in the field of entertainment they were not in the same genre and the two are easily distinguishable as serio-comic/actor and comic singer/composer, and the 'other' Harry as a classical conductor and composer.

Harry Braham has another legacy which has caused an intriguing mystery in the family to this day – and that is of what happened to 'Harry's Boys'.

When Harry was in England from 1895-1899, legend has it that he fell in love with a mulatto woman and that they had two sons.

Photographs of the boys as babies and toddlers exist, but their names and that of their mother are unknown. The family did at one point have pictures of them as teenagers, but these are now lost. The boys would have been the right age to fight in World War I, and – if they survived – to subsequently suffer the Spanish flu pandemic of 1918.

They were always known in the family as 'Harry's Boys'. If they did survive, perhaps they had children of their own, so maybe somewhere Harry's legacy does, in fact, live on ...

APPENDICES

Harry Braham's Articles on the Film Industry

New York Clipper, **17 February 1912:**

The moving picture companies are a national institution, and have come to stay for all time, and yet they are only in their infancy. The rapid strides film has made since its inception are remarkable, and it is not yet twenty years ago since London saw the first moving picture at the Empire, Leicester Square. Of course the pictures exhibited then were small and not to be compared with the life-sized figures of to-day. A very able article appeared in this journal some time back comparing the American pantomimists with the French and Italian. I absolutely endorse everything my *confrere* said in that article. The Latin races are born pantomimists, but a great change has come over the scene. The American and English speaking people want natural gesticulation, and the art of acting is to be natural, so to-day we are getting clean comedy and drama. The slap-stick and the monkey antics of the last decade are fast disappearing and instead of the foreign film being in demand, it is the American article that is in use in every country under the sun.

The time is not far distant when stars of the first magnitude will pose and star in parts made popular by them, and why not? No actor, be he great or small, should look down on the film actor. There are hundreds of idle Thespians only too glad to get that five dollar bill daily, especially in these days when theatrical engagements are so difficult to obtain most of the big companies have the stock company, consisting of twenty or more people, who receive good salaries for fifty two weeks in the year. These companies have several stage directors, many of whom are capable of staging the elaborate production seen on the stages of the Broadway theatres. These gentlemen not only tell and show the actor stage business, but they also teach them how to utilize their facial muscles. The stage carpenter in those companies must be a master craftsman, and what he doesn't know about building up scenes at short notice is not worth knowing. Then they have their property men coupled with a large wardrobe for the actor's use, grease paints, powder, cosmetics; in fact everything appertaining to an actor's art of make-up is at his disposal, free of cost. Should the actor be employed all day his meals are prepared for him gratuitously and served in the studio to see a director marshaling his forces with the megaphone is something to remember. Of course, the director likes best to have the actor of experience instead of the lay figure of the deadwood type, but at times he is compelled to take the outsider for a special type he needs. A short rehearsal takes place prior to taking the picture, when all is in readiness the camera does the rest, and it surely does not lie. The studios are brilliantly illuminated with all the latest improvements that the human brain can invent. An actor may play nightly, say before one thousand people, but the moving picture actor, perhaps the same night, is playing to a hundred thousand, from Maine to California, to the Antipodes, the Orient, and Europe thrown in, so the picture actor becomes popular the whole world over.

New York Dramatic Mirror, 30 April 1913

It is about twenty years ago since a well-known French actor M. Treury brought from France the "Cinematograph" to the Empire Theatre, Leicester Square, London, England. This was the inception of the motion picture before an Anglo-Saxon audience. The picture was small, and naturally the figures: also it was very unsteady. But for all these defects it was the commencement of a national amusement, and was voted by the press and public an enormous success.

What wonderful strides the moving pictures have made since then! There is not a city, town, or village to the four points of the compass that hasn't one or two moving picture houses. It matters not what language is spoken, the moving picture depicts in pantomime what words should convey. The Latin races have always been masters in the art of pantomime and for many years they held sway everywhere. Their pictures were in great demand, but the public gradually got tired of the knockabout ballet-stunts and slapstick comedy. They wanted a higher class entertainment.

American managers, always on the alert, diagnosed the pulse of the people and set to work to remedy the shortcomings of the actors and film makers of Europe. They commenced to build palatial studios, engaged reputable actors and actresses: also stage-managers of experience, and then moulded them for the American picture field. Indeed, I might say, it is very seldom that even an experienced legitimate stage-manager makes a good director, and the same may be said for actors. He might be one of the very best in the business, and yet absolutely fail at the picture work. One must serve an apprenticeship for the screen. He must use his facial muscles and gesticulate in pantomime, just as if he were speaking. A great actor once gave an aspirant to histrionic honors this advice: "My boy," said he, "always talk with your face". So to-day the American film is preeminent the world over.

Now a word about the moving picture actor, who has taken so kindly to this new field of work. A theatrical company engages an actor for the run of the piece – meaning a season's work. Of course, he has to take chances with the management. He first rehearses not less than four weeks, interlaced with several dress-rehearsals, some taking twelve hours, for which he doesn't get one cent. Then there is that iniquitous two weeks' clause in the contract that his services may be dispensed with at short notice. In fact, the contract is all for the party of the first part and nothing for the party of the second part. So where does the equity come in? If the piece is a hit, and he doesn't get discharged, his season may last twenty-five weeks; but if you sign with one of the big film companies, for the stock, you get a weekly stipend for fifty-two weeks in the year. No burning the midnight oil, no study, no wardrobe to supply. Everything is found for you – make up, consisting of all shades of grease paints, powders, crape hair, cosmetics, soap, and towels, and if you are made up before luncheon, you partake of the latter, free of cost in the studio. This applies to outdoor scenes also. The menu consists of soup, meat, vegetables, and liquids. The dressing rooms are large, well ventilated, and lighted by electricity. Furthermore, a film company is a happy democratic family.

The studio is a counterpart of the regular stage without footlights, and is not raised, being on a level with the floor. It is brilliantly lighted, looking for all the world like intense sun-shine. The difference between the regular stage and the moving picture rehearsal, is that the stage-manager, or author of the legitimate, reads his play to the company, after which the parts are handed out and a rehearsal takes place. Business of the piece is written in. This goes on until the actors are conversant with their lines, then parts are discarded, and the real acting takes place: for it is impossible to feel a part until such time that one is dead-letter perfect. The moving picture rehearsals are vastly different. The director calls his company around him, and with scenario in hand calls the ladies and gentlemen by their names, first mentioning what the wordless play is "Mr. ___ you are a lover, Miss ___, you are his affianced bride. Mrs. ___, you are the mother, Mr. ___, you are the father, Mr. ___, you are the villain", and so on. Thus the different scenes are rehearsed without parts, the director explaining the business, and, as the playlet proceeds, he elaborates and builds up situations and sensations that the author never dreamed of. The following is a scenario:

'The Long Lost Brother'. Scene – *Interior of Cottage. Door right. Window right of center. Door center. Fireplace left.*

Cashier of Works returning home with the men's wages, being unable to put the money in the bank on account of the bank being closed. His wife, sitting at the table (center), sewing with two small children (boy and girl) sitting at her feet. Wife rises at entrance of husband through door (center). They embrace. Children run up and kiss their father. Father hangs coat on peg at side of door (center,) also muffler and hat, then warms his hands at fire and stands before it (fireplace).

Well, dear, I am home sooner than usual. Should have been detained at bank counting the $3,000, but the bank closes on time, so have had to bring this *(touching bag of money)* home for safe-keeping until tomorrow, pay day, So here goes dear, to place it away for safe-keeping for the night. Nobody but ourselves has any idea so large an amount is secreted in so humble a place as mine *(Speaking with wife and children).* Now, you go to bed. (*Wife embraces husband and children kiss their father).* There is no need of you waiting for me, as I have several things to do before I can follow you. *(He goes to the door of the room (right) and closes it very carefully after them then he sits down and thinks.* If I could only be worth $3,000. Nobody would possibly suspect that I took it. *(Pointing to bureau where the money is)*. I could easily send a message to the wife to say that I was detained with a sick friend, and when all are asleep I could easily get into this place and take the money. I'll do it. *(Puts on coat, hat and muffler, opens door, blows out candle, closes door and departs in the night). Loud knocking is heard at the door. Wife appears, sees room vacant, and listens to the knocking Voice outside:* "Please let me in". *Wife:* "Who are you?" "I am Jack's long-lost brother". *Wife:* "Why, he's been dead years". "No, Jane, I am alive. I have been in Australia and have returned to see you all". *Wife opens door, puts candle in face and recognizes Jack's brother. She closes door and they sit down to table (center). They talk and seem pleased at the reunion, when another knock is heard. She opens door, messenger boy with letter (for Mrs Mason),* "Why, it is from Jack stating that he may not be home all night". *She sighs, then sits:* "Well, you must have a bite to eat, and then I will do my best to make you comfortable for the night." *She lays cloth on table and goes to larder and gets bread, cheese, and a bottle of beer. He eats and talks with his mouth full. After repast she excuses herself and goes through door (right). He takes pipe out and fills it with tobacco from his pouch and lights up. She returns smiling as much as to say* "All is ready". *He arises and follows her and closes door after him. (Room dark). Window is slowly opened and a man with a mask, dark lantern, appears. Cautiously gets from the window, listens at door (right), goes left and then opens bureau with key. After taking out money, is about to exit when the door (right) suddenly opens. Husband's wife and brother appear at door: the brother with six-shooter calls out:* "Hold up your hands". *Wife rushes forward, tears off the mask and exclaims:* "My God, my husband!". *Charles:* "My God, my brother!"

The prices for these pieces range from $25 up. They have to be sent to the studio, marked "Scenario Department" and a stamped envelope inclosed. The best way is to register them, and if the scenario is accepted, a check is forwarded to the author. Of course, a delay in some cases of many weeks takes place. The author signs a paper, and gives the company all right to the play.

A reel is one thousand feet of film: this being a short playlet. Some of the dramas take three thousand feet. Sara Bernhardt, in *Camille*, was a three-reel picture. This really constitutes an evening's entertainment, or nearly so.

There are what you term regulars, meaning actors and actresses out of employment, who apply at the studios for work. If their line is known by the director, and when he is in want of extra people, they are admitted to the studio, and told what to make-up, ready for their services. Whether they rehearse or go on in a scene, or are detained in the studio all day, they get $5. If a special part they get more: for the director is very liberal, if he or she is the particular type he needs. I might here remark that $5 is a god-send to the out-of-work Thespian when engagements are difficult to procure. Some days outside the studio there are hundreds of people (even such as are not actors) looking for a job. For the news flies like wildfire when there is going to be a big military, Indian, or Western drama to be produced. The "people" are selected by the director's lieutenant (who is more than courteous to all concerned). He takes their names and addresses in case they may be needed for more than one day – for some of these big pictures take a week or more.

First, the director takes the indoor scenes, and then come the outdoor daylight pictures. New Jersey supplies still-life of all kinds, and most of the companies go there. The entire company, with auxiliaries, meet at the ferry selected – say at 8.10am (weather permitting), and when they get off the boat the cars take them to the location selected. There is generally a very good hotel, and several rooms are reserved for dressing purposes. Those that are unaccustomed to make up are properly looked after and made up by experts. In the studio, when the scenes are ready, the people are called and a thorough rehearsal takes place. When the work is to take place in the open, automobiles take the people to the scene of the action. It is really surprising how the director, with the eyes of an eagle, sees instantly any defects in posing or grouping: for to keep a large number of people in action, as well as the principal characters (who depict in dumb show the story of the scenario) is no easy matter. The director, with a megaphone, calls the actors by their names, tells them the business of the piece, and what to do in facial expressions: "Miss So and So, do this! Smile! Open your eyes!" Mr So and So, your beard is not straight!" So you can see that the director's position is anything but an easy one. And the great secret of a director's success is to keep his temper.

When all is in readiness for the actual picture to be taken, you hear the words "We'll take it!" It is the rule to take two pictures of each scene. The way scenes are built inside the studio seems fairy-like to the beholder. They grow so rapidly before your eyes. The master carpenter, assistants, and electricians are the best craftsmen that stageland can procure.

It takes three or four weeks before a picture is released by the censor. Most of the big companies have studios out in California, and when Winter arrives, like birds of passage, they migrate to that sunny country to stay there not less than six months. Here no electricity is needed for indoor work, old Sol supplying it free of cost.

Just to show how popular the world over the picture actor has become, I may mention that recently a well-known comedian was sent to England to impersonate some of the characters of Charles Dickens. No sooner had he arrived than he was recognized and followed about the streets of London by hundreds of people. Most of the big London dailies gave him articles headed "the most popular actor in the world". For an actor may play on the legitimate stage before a thousand people nightly, but a "movie" will play before a hundred thousand.

The motion pictures are to-day, as I said before, a national institution, and have come to stay for all time, and yet they are only in the embryo: for in the not distant future symphony orchestras, consisting of one hundred performers, will accompany this most remarkable industry.

In London, the picture theater managers charge for admission 6 pence, 1 shilling, 2 shillings, 3 shillings, and some as high as 4 shillings. Most of these houses serve gratis what the English term the "4 o'clock tea" with thin bread and butter and cake. Outside the regular theaters, and music halls, there are many moving picture theaters, all doing a land office business. The attendants are generally dressed in livery.

I was appearing in London a few years ago, and the three big theatres of varieties were: The Alhambra, the Empire and the Palace. Of course the Alhambra and the Empire did the big business. The Palace was originally built for an English Opera House; but like the

Hammerstein's pet hobby, singularly failed. It always had the best talent that the market could supply, and yet this beautiful theater was not a success. The American picture companies stepped in the breach, was headliner, and ever since then the house has been crowded.

King George gave his patronage and presence, recently, to a matinee for some charitable institution, when all the stars of the vaudeville firmament appeared. This alone shows what prestige the Palace now holds in the estimation of a loyal but conservative English public.

The American film director has revolutionized the motion pictures, for there is not any department connected with the screen line of work which they are not conversant. In directing a scenario they are cool, logical, and polite to their companies. This being the acme of stage management, it is rather late in the day for me to tell the American people what the Yankee films have done and are doing. I really believe these gentlemen take fairy tales and turn them into tragedies or comedies, for their imagination and discernment are unsurpassed. Great stage producers are born, not made.

A Literary Curiosity

Harry Braham also dabbled in poetry and wrote this for *The New York Clipper*, 17 February 1912, combining lines from poets and writers including Dr Johnson, Pope, Spencer, Longfellow, Byron, Smollett, Milton, Churchill and many others:

Why all this toil for triumphs of an hour?
Life's a short Summer, man a flower.
By turns we catch the vital breath and die -
The cradle and the tomb, alas so nigh.
To be is better far than not to be,
Though all man's life may seem a tragedy:
But light cares speak when mighty griefs are dumb
The bottom is but shallow, whence they come,
Your fate is but the common fate of all:
Unmingled joys here to no man befall,
Nature to each allots his proper sphere:
Fortune makes folly her peculiar care:
Custom does not reason overrule,
And throws a cruel Sunshine on a fool.
Live well; how long or short, permit to heaven:
They who forgive most shall be most forgiven -
Sin may be clasped so close that we cannot see its face-
Vile intercourse where virtue has no place,
Then keep each passion down, however dear,
Thou pendulum betwixt a smile and tear:
Her sensual snares, let faithless pleasures lay,
With craft and skill, to ruin and betray,

Soar not too high to fall, but stoop to raise,
We masters grow of all that we despise,
O, when I renounce that impious self-esteem:
Riches have wings, and grandeur is a dream,
Think not ambition wise because 'tis brave,
The paths of glory lead but to the grave,
What is ambition? – 'tis a glorious cheat!
Only destruction to the brave and great,
What's all the gaudy glitter of a crown?
The way to bliss lies not on beds of down,
How long we live, not years but actions tell,
That man lives twice who lives the first life well,
Make then, while yet we may, your God your friend
When Christians worship, yet not comprehend:
The trust that's given, guard, and to yourself be just:
For, live we how we can, yet die we must.

Music Halls at which Harry Braham Appeared

LONDON

Alhambra, Leicester Square. Opened as Royal Panopticon of Science and Art in 1854; converted in 1858 and 1860; destroyed by fire in 1882; rebuilt in 1883; demolished 1936 and replaced by Odeon cinema

Bedford, Camden High St. Built in 1861 as part of tea gardens to the Bedford Arms public house; demolished in 1898

Cambridge, Commercial St, Shoreditch. Opened in 1864; destroyed by fire in 1896

Canterbury, Westminster Bridge Rd. First ever music hall opened in 1852; reconstructed into a three-tier theatre in 1876; destroyed by bombing in World War II in 1942

Collins, Islington. Conversion of Lansdowne Arms pub by Irish vocalist Sam Collins; bought by a syndicate in 1863; remodeled in 1897; mostly destroyed by fire in 1958 apart from façade and walls; now forms part of Waterstone's bookstore

Crystal Palace, Hyde Park. Built in 1851 for Great Exhibition; moved to Sydenham Hill in 1852 where it was opened by Queen Victoria in 1854; destroyed by fire in 1936

Deacons, Myddelton Place, Finsbury. Built in 1861; demolished in 1891

Duke Of Connaught, Woolwich. 33 New Road Woolwich Built 1881 flat floored concert room above Duke of Connaught Coffee Tavern, after alterations to variety theatre and Woolwich picture palace, demolished 1980s

Gattis in the Road, Westminster Bridge Road. Built in 1865; damaged during World War II demolished in **1950**

Gattis under the Arches, Villiers St, Charing Cross. Built in 1863; demolished in 1980s; now rebuilt as the Charing Cross Theatre

Kensington Music Hall, Kensington Park Road. Opened 1870

Lusby's, Mile End Road. Opened around 1848 as Eagle Public House; replaced by Lusby's Summer and Winter Garden, then Music Hall; destroyed by fire in 1884

Marylebone, Marylebone High St. Opened in 1856 by Sam Collins; in business until 1900

Metropolitan, Edgware Rd, Paddington. Built on site of White Lion Pub in 1836; subsequently Turnhams Grand Concert Hall; opened as music hall in 1864; reconstructed in 1897; demolished in 1963

Oxford Music Hall, Oxford St. Opened in 1861; damaged by fire in 1868; re-opened in 1869; damaged again by fire in 1872; re-opened in 1873; demolished in 1892

Paragon, Mile End Road. Formerly Lusby's (destroyed by fire in 1884); rebuilt as Paragon in 1885; demolished in 1912

Pavilion, Whitechapel Road, Stepney. Opened in 1827; destroyed by fire in 1856; rebuilt in 1874; damaged by bombing in World War II; demolished in 1962

Queens Arms Palace of Varieties, Poplar High St. Built in 1856; reconstructed in 1898; demolished in 1964

Raglan, Union St, Shoreditch. Built in 1840s; repeatedly destroyed by fire; rebuilt in 1872; destroyed by fire in 1883

Royal Music Hall, High Holborn. Originally named Westons Music Hall in 1857; renamed Royal Music Hall in 1868; altered by Frank Matcham in 1906; became Holborn Empire; bombed in 1941; demolished in 1960

South London Palace of Varieties, London Road, Lambeth. Built in 1869; closed in 1940; damaged by World War II bombing in 1941; demolished in 1955

Star Music Hall, Abbey St, Bermondsey. Built in 1867 as part of Star and Garter pub; closed in 1919; reopened as Star cinema; demolished in 1963

Sun, Knightsbridge High St. Built in 1851; demolished in 1930s

The Temple of Varieties, King St, Hammersmith. Built in 1880 as town hall; renamed Temple of Varieties; altered in 1898 by Frank Matcham; converted to a cinema in 1930s; demolished in 1950

Town Hall, Shoreditch. Built in 1865; after many alterations, building still in use

Trocadero, Piccadilly Circus. Converted in 1882 from Argyll Rooms; closed in 1894; now multi-entertainment venue

Welsh Harp, Hendon. Conversion of Old Welsh Harp Pub in 1859; demolished in 1970; reservoir still named Welsh Harp

Regional Music Halls and Theatres

Aberdeen – Grand Concert Hall

Aberdeen – McFarlands Music Hall

Belfast – Alhambra. Built in 1871; destroyed by fire then rebuilt in 1879; destroyed by fire and demolished in 1959

Birkenhead – Prince of Wales Theatre. Built in 1868 as the Argyle Theatre, renamed as Prince of Wales in 1876 reverting to the Argyle in 1890; first theatre to broadcast radio shows to the Commonwealth and USA by shortwave radio, also showed footage of King Edward VII funeral in 1910. Sir Harry Lauder, Dan Leno, Bud Flanagan and Charlie Chaplin appeared here; destroyed during the Battle of Britain in World War II

Birmingham – Days Crystal Palace. On site of pub The White Swan, corner of Smallbrook St and Hurst St; built in 1862 by James Day; closed in 1893; sold to Moss Empires; opened as New Empire Theatre of Varieties in 1894; damaged by World War II bombing in 1941; demolished in 1951

Birmingham – Theatre Royal, New St. Built in 1774; altered through the years; rebuilt and altered again in 1875 by Archibald

Naden; rebuilt again in 1885; demolished in 1902 including the 1770s façade

Brighton – Aquarium. Opened in 1872; still in use though altered

Brighton – Eden Theatre, North Road. Built between1891-1894; renamed Grand Theatre; closed in 1955; damaged by fire in 1961 and demolished

Brighton – Grand Concert Hall, Church St. Opened 1867; remodeled 1935; still in use as The Dome Concert Hall

Brighton – Oxford Music Hall, New Road. Opened in 1863; destroyed by fire in 1867; rebuilt in 1868; closed in 1891; rebuilt and renamed Bright Empire and the Dolphin Theatre; demolished in 1967

Chatham – Kent Barnards, High St. Destroyed by fire in 1886; rebuilt as Barnards New Palace of Varieties; damaged again by fire in 1900; destroyed by fire in 1934

Dundee – Dundee Music Hall. Opened in Shore St as an Exchange in 1828 then as Music Hall in 1866 William McFarland operated it as Dundee Music Hall (and Opera House) until 1888 leased to John Young who renamed it the Excelsior, in 1889 building was altered inside removing balcony, stage gallery and boxes, became Masonic Temple now in use as Shore Youth Venue

Dundee – Her Majesty's Theatre Seagate. Opened 1885 by William McFarland, then leased to Robert Arthur; sold as a picture house named The Majestic; rebuilt during 1930s; demolished during World War II; Lloyds Bar now on its site

145

Edinburgh – Moss Theatre of Varieties, Chambers St. Built by Edward Moss in 1875; closed 1892

Edinburgh –Theatre Royal, Broughton St. Built in 1876; demolished in 1946 after successive fires and rebuilds

Glasgow – Britannia Music Hall, Trongate. Built in 1857; in use as music hall from 1859-1938; used as shop and warehouse; now a conservation project including shows

Glasgow – Browns Music Hall, Dunlop St. Opened in 1853; closed in 1887

Glasgow – Gaiety Theatre, Sauchiehall St. Built in 1874; demolished in 1897; new theatre built on the site named Empire Theatre; demolished 1963 – now office block Empire House – where I began my career

Glasgow – Star Music Hall, Watson St Glasgow Cross. Opened in 1878; refurbished as Shakespeare Music Hall by Arthur Lloyd; eventually became Pringles Picture Palace; destroyed by fire in 1952

Great Yarmouth – Aquarium, Marine Parade. Opened in 1876; now used as a nightclub and cinema

Leicester – Paul's Hall of Varieties, Belgrave Gate/Wilton St. Originally The Old Cheese Pub; song and supper room added in 1864; renamed the Midland Music Hall 1870; rebuilt 1876; destroyed by fire 1889

Liverpool – Saunders Theatre Of Varieties, Paradise Street. Opened 1850 as The Royal Colosseum and Music Hall a conversion of Unitarian Chapel originally built 1791, taken over by Dan Saunders 1880, renamed City Theatre of Varieties, Grand Theatre, then Grand Theatre and Opera House. Mostly demolished 1903 retaining frontage and side walls, rebuilt as Queens Theatre, renamed Kelly's Theatre. Closed 1916 used as warehouse bombed during World War II then demolished

Liverpool – Star, Williamson Square. Built in 1866; now in use as Playhouse Theatre

Lynn – Athenaeum Concert Hall

Manchester – Folly. Built in 1865; reconstructed in 1897 and 1921 as a cinema; destroyed by fire and demolished in 1936

Manchester – Great St James' Hall, Oxford St. Built 1884; closed 1907; reopened as theatre 1908; demolished 1912

Manchester – Tivoli Theatre – see Folly Theatre

Northampton – Prince of Wales Concert Hall Gold St Opened 1855 as a music hall part of Crow and Horseshoe Inn, renamed Alhambra Music Hall, Star Hall of Varieties, Theatre of Varieties and Palace Theatre of Varieties, subsequently The Palace Vaudeville Theatre, The Picture House, Vint's Palace, Vint's Picture Palace, The Majestic Cinema -demolished 1950previously Theatre of Varieties

Plymouth – St Andrews Music Hall

Portsmouth – Royal Amphitheatre, Gunwharf Rd/St Mary's St – see South of England Music Hall

147

Portsmouth – Princes Theatre, Lake Road. Opened in 1869; closed in 1872; rebuilt and remodeled, opening again the same year; destroyed by fire in 1882

Portsmouth. South of England Music Hall St Mary's St Originally built 1854 on the site of The Blue Bell Inn; reportedly held 2000 people lit by gas and heated by 16 fires; became Alhambra, New South of England Grand Palace, and Barnards Royal Amphitheatre; caught fire in 1878 and again in 1890; demolished

Preston – Gaiety Theatre, Tithebarn St. Opened 1882; destroyed by fire 1900 and reopened the same year as the New Prince's Theatre; demolished 1964

Ramsgate – Harp Music Hall

Australian Music Halls and Theatres

Adelaide – Theatre Royal, Hindley St. Opened in 1868; demolished in 1878

Bathurst – Lewis's Pavilion

Benalla – St George's Hall

Brisbane – School of Arts, corner of Queen St and Creek St. Opened in 1864; sold to National Bank in 1872; continued use as School of Arts until 1878, demolished

Brisbane – Victoria Theatre, Elizabeth St. Opened in 1865 as Mason's concert hall; underwent various name changes such as Theatre Royal, Victoria Theatre and Royal Victoria Theatre; demolished in 1880

Home Rule – Royal Shamrock Theatre

Melbourne – Apollo Music Hall, Bourke St. Built 1862, contained with Haymarket Theatre as a complex; roller-skating introduced in 1866; site occupied as Eastern arcade and demolished

Melbourne – St George's Hall, Bourke St. Opened in 1860s; demolished and rebuilt as De Hoyts Theatre in 1914

Sydney – Café Chantant, York St. Built in 1850; opened as Circus Royal; re-opened as theatre in 1869, as Theatre Royal briefly and then Queens Theatre in 1873 after rebuild; rebuilt and refurbished again in 1875; closed in 1882

Sydney – Exhibition Hall

Sydney – Masonic Hall, York St. Built in 1853; demolished 1908

Sydney – School of Arts, Pitt St. Founded in 1833 as Sydney Mechanical School of Arts; now in use as The Arthouse Hotel

West Maitland – Olympic Theatre, Main St. Opened in 1859; demolished in 1893

West Maitland – School of Arts

New Zealand Theatres

Auckland – Prince of Wales Theatre, previously Brunswick Music Hall unknown

Christchurch – Canterbury Music Hall, Gloucester St. Built in 1861; demolished in 1876

Christchurch – Oddfellows Hall, Lichfield St. Built in 1860; building was moved to Disraeli St Addington in 1903; now a coffee house

Dunedin – Princess Theatre. Built in 1862; destroyed by fire in 1875

Dunedin – Queens Theatre, Princes St. Built in 1862

Wellington – Theatre Royal, Johnston St. Built in 1873; closed in 1911

US Theatres

NEW YORK CITY

Academy of Music, East 14th St and Irving Place. Opened 1866: demolished 1926

Amphion, 43rd St and Bedford Ave. Opened approx 1888; demolished 1940

Daly's, 1221 Broadway. Opened as Banvards Museum 1867; Demolished 1920

Eden Musee, 55 West 23rd St. Opened 1884; closed and demolished 1915

Grand Opera House, 8th Ave and 23rd St. Formerly Pikes Opera House, opened 1868; demolished 1960

Harlem Opera House, 211 West 125th St. Opened 1889; demolished

Hyde and Behman's Theatre, Fulton St Brooklyn. Opened 1877, later Olympic and Tivoli Theatre; closed 1952; demolished 1954

Koster and Bials Concert Hall, 23rd St. Opened 1879; part remains of beer garden which was attached to the hall called 'The Corner'

Maxine Elliotts, 109 West 39th St. Opened 1908; demolished 1960

Montauk, Fulton St, Brooklyn. Opened 1895 as New Montauk Theatre. Theatre was entirely moved a few hundred yards in 1907 to make way for the Flatbush Ave Extension; demolished in 1940

Park Theatre, Fulton St. Opened 1863; demolished 1908

Pastor's Theatre, 585 Broadway originally Michael Leavitt's Theatre. Opened 1874; demolished

151

People's Theatre, 199-201 Bowery. Originally Hoyms Theatre, built 1858 then Tony Pastor's Opera House opened 1865-1875; burnt and rebuilt 1883 as Miner's Peoples Theatre; demolished 1945

Poole's Theatre, 8th St and fourth Ave formerly Church of St Ann's. Built 1871, later known as Germania Theatre; demolished 1903

Tony Pastor

Star Theatre, Broadway and 13th St. Formerly Wallacks, built 1860; demolished 1901

Tammany Hall – Tony Pastor's, 14th St. Previously Germania Theatre leased by Tony 1881; demolished 1928

Other US Cities

Anaconda, Montana – Margaret Theatre, 305 Main St. Built 1897; destroyed 1929

Baltimore, Maryland – Holliday Street Theatre. Opened 1873; after a couple of fires, demolished 1917

Bangor, Maine – Opera House, Main St. Opened 1882; destroyed by fire 1914

Boston, Massachusetts – Columbia Theatre, 978 Washington St. Built 1891; demolished 1957

Boston, Massachusetts – Hollis Street Theatre Opened 1885; demolished 1953

Boston, Massachusetts – Howard Athaeneum, 34 Howard St Opened 1846; demolished 1953

Boston, Massachusetts – Park Theatre, Washington St Opened 1879; demolished 1990

Bridgeport, Connecticut – theatre unknown

Butte, Montana – Grand Family Theatre, North Montana St. Opened 1901; demolished 1980s

Carbondale, Pennsylvania – theatre unknown

Chicago, Illinois – Opera House West, Washington Ave N Clark St. Built 1884-85; demolished 1912

Decatur, Illinois – Powers Grand Opera House, North East corner South Water and Wood Streets. Built 1889; burned 1914

Des Moines, Iowa – Empire Theatre

Detroit, Michigan – Opera House, Campus Martius Park. Built 1869; demolished 1963

Duluth, Minnesota – Metropolitan Opera House The Bowery. Opened 1902; demolished 1910

Duluth, Minnesota – Bijou Theatre 12 East Superior Street Built 1903 became Empress Theatre 1911 damaged by fire 1915 building still stands as retail shop

Eau Claire, Wisconsin – Grand Opera House, Barstow Main and River (Graham) Streets. Built 1883; demolished 1938

Fargo, North Dakota – Grand Family Theatre, 622 First Avenue North. Opened 1906; closed 1927. After a fire and remodeling, demolished 1970s

Honolulu, Hawaii – Royal Hawaiian Theatre. Opened 1848; demolished 1881

Newark, New Jersey – Proctors, Market St. Opened 1895; remodelled as Proctors Palace Theatre and later Penthouse Cinema, a rare double decker theatre; still exists though abandoned

New Haven, Connecticut – Hyperion: College and Chapel St. Built 1880; demolished 1998

Marlboro, Massachusetts – theatre unknown

Minneapolis, Minnesota – Hennepin Avenue Theatre

Minneapolis, Minnesota – Unique Theatre, 520 Hennepin Avenue. Built 1904; demolished 1930s

New Bedford, Massachusetts – New Bedford Theatre, 249

Union St. Built 1896; demolished 1967

Oakland, California – MacDonough Theatre, 1320 Broadway. Opened 1892; demolished 1956

Philadelphia, Pennsylvania – Arch Street Theatre, 609-615 Arch St. Built 1826; demolished 1936

Philadelphia, Pennsylvania – Fox's American Theatre 809 Walnut Street. Built 1863; burned and rebuilt 1867; burned 1892

Philadelphia, Pennsylvania – National Theatre, 824-836 Chestnut St. Built 1851; demolished

Pittsfield, Massachusetts – theatre unknown

Providence Rhode Island – theatre unknown

San Francisco, California – Alcazar, 116 O'Farrell St. Built 1885; destroyed earthquake and fire 1906

San Francisco, California – Bella Union Theatre, Portsmouth Square. Built 1868; destroyed earthquake and fire 1906

San Francisco, California – Bush Street Theatre. Destroyed earthquake and fire

San Francisco, California – Chutes, 10th Ave and Fulton. Part of recreation park, built 1895; demolished 1911

San Francisco, California – Fischers.

San Francisco, California – National Theatre.

San Francisco, California – Orpheum, 1631 Ellis St near Fillmore. Opened Jan 1907, later renamed Garrick Theatre; demolished 1970s

Seattle Washington – Star Theatre, Madison St. Built 1905; demolished 1971

Spokane Washington – Washington Theatre, 249 W Riverside Ave. Built 1906/07, renamed Empress then Studio; demolished 1982

St Louis Missouri – Theatre Comique

St Paul Minnesota – Metropolitan Opera House, 100 East 6th St. Built 1890; demolished 1936

Syracuse, New York – Wieting Opera House, Clinton Square. Built 1897; demolished

Troy, New York – Griswold Opera House, 12 Third St. Built 1871; burned 1950s

Troy, New York – Proctor's, Fourth Street. Built 1914, double balcony theatre; currently abandoned

Washington, DC – New National Theatre, Pennsylvania Ave. Opened 1835; reconstructed several times; still in use

Canada

Toronto – Grand Opera House, Adelaide Street West. Opened 1874; demolished 1927

Victoria BC – New Grand Theatre

Winnipeg – Bijou Theatre, 498 Main St. Opened 1904; closed 1956; burned down 1979

Germany

Berlin – Staatsoper, Unter Den Linden. Built 1742; destroyed World War II and rebuilt to original design

Hamburg – theatre unknown

Jamaica

Kingston – Theatre Royal. Built 1860s; destroyed by earthquake 1907

Spanish Town, Montego Bay, Port Maria, Annotto Bay. – theatres unknown

SOURCES

Books:

Anderson, Gae. *Tivoli King: The Life of Harry Rickards, Vaudeville Showman*, Allen and Unwin 2009

Bowers, Judith. *Stan Laurel and Other Stars of the Panopticon: The Story of The Britannia Music Hall*, Berlinn 2007

Brown, Karl. *Adventures with DW Griffith*, Faber and Faber, 1988

Crane, William H. *Footprints and Echoes*, EP Dutton, 1927

Fields, Armond. *Tony Pastor, Father of Vaudeville*, McFarland and Co, 2011

Flanders, Judith. *The Victorian City, Everyday life in Dickens' London*, Atlantic, 2013

Gillies, Midge. *Marie Lloyd, The One and Only*, Gollanz, 2001

MacQueen-Pope, Walter James. *The Melodies Linger On*, WH Allen, 1935

Maloney, Paul. *Scotland and The Music Hall*, Manchester University Press, 2003

Picard, Liza. *Victorian London: The Life of A City 1840 -1870*, Phoenix, 2006

Libraries and internet:

Ancestry.co.uk and Ancestry.com
Arthurlloyd.co.uk
Australian Variety Theatre Archive
Bodleian Library
British Library Newspaper Archive
Chronicling America

FamilyLink
FultonHistory.com
National Library of Australia
Newspaperarchive.com
New York Times Archive
Paperspast, New Zealand
Staten Island Museum
Trove, National Library of Australia
Wikipedia

ACKNOWLEDGEMENTS

Gae Anderson (no relation), James Lyle and Joan Anderson, K Kevyne Baar, Henryk Behnke, Judith Bowers, Julia Brown (neé Cane-Honeysett) Rosanna Brown, John Calhoun, Laurence, Mary and Tony Cane-Honeysett, Maureen Chapman-Towns, Sally Chestnutt, Peter Court, Cara Dellatte, Clay Djubal, Alison, Donald and Matthew Farmer, Graham Hodson, Graham Hunter, Molly Keener, Gaby Laws, Kevin Leamon, Martin Lee, Matthew Lloyd, Nancy Hines, Gail Malmgreen, Anna Meyer, Rebecca Petersen, John Strohl, Jill Sullivan, Clare Tally Foos, Tom Tryniski, Max Tyler, Chelsea Weathers, Rosemary Wilmot, and Linda C Wood − who started me on this journey. To anyone I may have inadvertently missed, my sincere apologies.

And last but by no means least, my editor Amanda Field whose guidance and patience has been incredible.

All photographs are from my own collection or are in the public domain, with the exception of the following, which are reproduced by kind permission of the organisations named: City Of Richmond Fire (British Newspaper archive); Frederick Burgess and Moore & Burgess Minstrels (Harry Ransom Center, The University of Texas at Austin); Thomas Pedder Hudson (Australian Variety Theatre Archive); Queens Theatre (State Library of New South Wales GP01-07042); School Of Arts (State Library of New South Wales GP01-05635); Lizzie Watson (State Library of New South Wales PXA 362/3/45); Britannia Music Hall (Britannia Music Hall Trust); Star Theatre (Picture Collection, The New York Public Library, Astor, Lenox and Tilden Foundations); Baron Ling Ching (Clarence Herbert New and Robert Warrington New Papers, MS577z, Smith Reynolds Library Special Collections and Archives, Wake Forest University, Winston-Salem, NC); 1907 Faces tour (University of Washington Libraries Special Collections UW29457); Actors Fund Home, Staten Island (The Collection of The Staten Island Museum); Charles and Edwin Braham (Mary Cane-Honeysett); Harry's Boys (Mary Cane-Honeysett); all song sheets apart from The Senator (Bodleian Library, Oxford).

INDEX

Index of people, acts, songs and productions

Ackland, Harry 35-36
A Great New York Fire 108
Alfred, Prince (son of Queen Victoria) 29, 32, 46
Allison, James 33
Always Washing 18
American Excelsior Minstrels 28-29
American Minister The 104
An Accidental Sweetheart 109
Arthur, Robert, 145
Athol (of Rowe and Athol) 85
At The Ball 41
A Trip To Paris 51

Baker, Charles T 47
Balloon, The 91, 93
Barnett, John 34
Barnett, JP 85
Barnum, PT 86
Barrett, George 85
Barrett, Mr, (Chief Officer, St Vincent) 22
Barrymore, Georgie Drew 88, 104
Bartle Frere, Sir Henry 63, 65
Barton, Sir Edmund 36
Bayless, L M 33, 57, 59
Bazalgette, Joseph 5
Beerbohm Tree, Sir Herbert 85
Beere, Mrs Bernard 85
Bernhardt, Sara 135

'Biron' (critic) 35, 36
Birth Of A Nation The 119, 121
Blanche, Mme (Mlle) 47
Bonaparte, Empress Eugenie 65
Bonaparte, Prince Louis Napoleon 65
Bonaparte, Emperor Napoleon III 65
Bonehill, Bessie 78
Booth, Agnes 104
Booth, John Wilkes 104, 107
Bowers, Judith *i*
Boy I Love Is Up In The Gallery, The 75
Boys Will Be Boys 124
Braham, Cecil 123
Braham, Charles 4, 19-20, 60, 108, 122
Braham, Edwin 4, 8, 55, 60, 101, 107-108, 117, 119
Braham, Nathaniel 2-8, 12, 16, 20, 55-56, 58-60, 96, 101, 107, 128
Braham, Susan 2-4, 7, 8, 10, 12, 56, 96, 101, 107
Braidwood, James 6
Brand, John *ii*
Branscombe, Arthur 106
Branscombe, William L 115
Brigham Young 28-29
Brown Potter, Mrs James 86
Browne, Walter 115

161

Burgess, Emma 10, 12
Burgess, Florence 12
Burgess, Frederick 9-12
Burgess, Washington 12
Burnaby, Frederick Gustavus 80-83
Burnaby The Brave 80-81
Byron, Lord 24, 139

Captain Jinks Of The Horse Marines 116
Carrotty Hair 28
Caunt, Benjamin 3
Caunt, Cornelius 3
Caunt, Martha 3
Cetshwayo, King 65
Champagne Charlie 78
Chaplin, Charlie 144
Chapman, Henry 41
Chelmsford, Lord 63, 65
Chillingowallabadorie 28
Christy, Edwin Pearce 8-9
Christy Minstrels 9-10, 13
Christy Minstrels, Royal 14, 16
Churchill 139
Clayton, John 85
Clegg, Tom 67
Cleveland, Grover 88
Cobb and Co 37
Coburn, Charles 75
Cody, William, (Buffalo Bill) 85
Colley, Edward 84
Collins, Abraham 83
Collins, Bella 67
Collins, Sam 141
Coyne, Fred 71
Crane, William Henry 88, 90-91, 93-94, 97, 102-105, 124

Curie, Marie 108
Cusick (of Pullas and Cusick) 67
Custer, General 55

Danger Signal, The 73-74
Darton, William, (Chief Officer) 99
Daughter Of The Regiment 38
Davis, J Charles 75
Delsarte, Francois 54
Dickens, Charles 13, 113, 115, 137
Dick Whittington 107
Didcott, Hugh Jay 79, 84, 86
Disraeli, Benjamin (1st Earl of Beaconsfield) 68
Dixon, Lizzie 35, 36
Dixon, Thomas Jr 120
Douglas, Alfred (Bosie) 77
Douglas, Francis 77
Douglas, John Sholto, (Marquess of Queensberry) 77
Dvorak, Antonin 13

Earle, Virginia 111
Edward VII, King 79, 144
Elliott, Maxine 151
Emerson, Billy 48, 50-51
Erlanger, AL 124
Everywoman 115

Fair One with the Golden Locks, The 92
Ferries, (Captain, Tartar) 49-50
Fight, The 119
Fish (of Fish and Ralston) 85
Flanagan, Bud 144

Foley, John 24
Foley, Kate 24
Forde, Florrie 32
For Money 103
Frece de, Lady, (Vesta Tilley) 71
Frece de, Walter 71
Fuller, La Louie (Marie Louise) 108, 109

George V, King 138
General Jinks 41
Gerry, Eldridge T Jr 94-95
Gilbert, Fred 61
Gilbert, WS 45
Gildard, Thomas *i, ii*
Gish, Lillian 120
Gladstone, William Ewart 68, 69
Gog (of Gog and Magog, Crystal Palace Giants) 42
Gone with the Wind 120
Goodbye My Love 51
Good Evening 29, 34
Gordon, General Charles George 83
Gounod, Charles 13
Graham, JL 85
Grey, Lily 75, 129-130
Grieg, Edvard 13
Griffith, DW 119, 121-122
Gunner, Samuel 73-74

Hamew, Mons 47
Hammerstein, Oscar 138
Happy Go Bill 29
Harry Braham, the Man with One Hundred Faces and Characters From Charles Dickens 113
Hart, Josh 116

Haydon, JS 80
Heads of Peculiar People We Meet, The 92
Heloise (of Rachel and Heloise) 41-42
Hertz, Carl 85
Hemingway, Henry 32, 67-69
Hewitt, Agnes 85
Hill, Jenny, (The Vital Spark) 60
Hill, William and Son 32
His Absent Boy 109
Holtermann, Bernhardt 43
Hoodman Blind 87, 93
Houdini, Harry 112-113
Howard, JH 92
Howarde, Lydia 35
Howson, Chas E 25
Hubner, Arthur *i*
Hudson, Thomas Pedder (Tommy) 18-19, 21-29, 33-37, 48, 126
Hunt, GW 46, 58
Hydes, Johnny 91

I'm A Lawyer, My Name Is Marks 69

Jackson, Enderby 29, 32-33, 116
Johnson, Dr Samuel 139
Jones, Henry Arthur 87
Jones, John G (Captain, Counsellor) 99

Kalakaua, David (King) 50-51, 93
Kamehemaha IV, King 50
Kaufmann (theatrical manager) 106

163

KCB 38-39
Kean, William *i*
Kelly, Ned 37
Keogh, George 86
Kiss When You Can 82
Klaw, Marcus 124
Kruger, Oom Paul 109

Langtry, Lily 86
La Rose, Harry 85
Lauder, Sir Harry 144
Laurel, Stan *ii*
Lautrec, Henri de Toulouse 108
Leete, Benjamin (Harry Rickards) 117
Leno, Dan 32, 78-79, 83, 128, 144
Leno, John Bedford 7
Lewis, JA 197
Leybourne, George 75, 78
Lincoln, Abraham 104
Lingard, William Horace 116
Lloyd, Arthur 60, 70, 74-75, 79, 146
Lloyd, David D 90
Lloyd, Marie 32, 75, 128
Loftus, Marie 74, 79, 83
Lovejoy, Mr (Chief Steward, St Vincent) 21
Louttitt, Alex (Captain, St Vincent) 22
Loyal, George 46
Lunaillo, William C 50

Mackaye, Steele 53, 88
Magic Melody 45
Magog (of Gog and Magog, Crystal Palace Giants) 42

Maguire, Tom 116
Masks and Faces 17, 76, 84, 94, 107, 112-113, 115
Matcham, Frank 143
Maynard, Ambrose 75
McAnthony and Chloe Pottra 88
McKinley, William 109
McCarthy, Charles 108
McFarland, William 61, 70, 144, 145
MacFarlane, Robert *i, ii*
Milton, John 139
Miss Springtime 124
Montague (of Wilsom and Montague) 13
Moore, George Washington (Pony) 10-12
Moore, John 85
Morocco Bound 106, 109
Morton, Charles 15, 84
Moses and Son 106
Moss, Edward 146
Moto, Yamo 38
Muir, Hugh *i, ii*

Naden, Archibald 144-145
Naughty Cupid 69
Newes, Major 85

O'Brien, Alex (Alick) 47
O'Farrell, Henry James 29
Old Toll House, The 92
Old Village Blacksmith Shop, The 72
On Probation 90, 93

Pain, Oliver 91
Papa Perrichon 93

164

Suppressed Evidence 119
Sutton, Charles 71
Sweeney (of Sweeney and Ryland) 85

Tambaroora Gold 27, 29
Tchaikovsky, Pyotr Ilyich 13
Tetlow, Samuel 53
Thackeray, William Makepeace 10
Thiodon, Aspinall 42
Thomson, Alexander (Greek) *i*
Tich, Little 128
Tilley, Vesta 71, 75, 78
Tolano, J 41
Took, JL 85
Torr, Sam 64
Treury, M 132

Ulma, Miss 85

Valentino, Rudolph 127
Vance, The Great, (Alfred Peck Stevens) 71, 78
Vengeance of Heaven 119
Victoria, Queen 13-14, 29, 83-84, 86, 126, 141

Walch, Garnet 45
Wall (Agents) 53
Warner, Charles 85
Washington, George 109
Watson, Lizzie 26, 29-38, 40-43, 45-62, 66-72, 74-75, 78-79, 83, 94, 115
- as Eliza Stephenson 32
- as Eliza Hemingway 83

Watt, James, (Captain, Lammermuir) 33
We Can't Be As Bad As All That 115
Whales Of August, The 120
Wheeler, Elizabeth 4
Wheeler, Thomas 4
White, George R 111-112
Wilde, Oscar 77
Wilder, Marshall P 86
Wild Horse Of Tartary, The 24
Wilhelm, Kaiser 109
Wilsom (of Wilsom and Montague) 13
Wilson, Barry 67
Wilson, Edward 4
Wilson, Nellie 85
Wilson Brothers 85
Wilson, Woodrow 120
Wodehouse, PG 124
Wolseley, Sir Garnet Joseph 62-65
Wood, Charlotte Selina (Little Tuesday) 94
Wood, Mrs John 85
Wu, Minister 109

Yemans, Lydia 85
Young, Brigham 28-29
Young, Chas 91
Young, John 145

Zulu, Madame 46

Parisian 'Arry 46, 75
Parker, Orville 85
Parkes, Hon Henry 34
Pastor, Tony 54, 58, 78, 84, 86, 130, 151-152
Paul Kauvar 88, 93
Piccadilly 28, 35, 51
Pickard, Albert Ernest *ii*
Pile, William and Co 21
Pope, Alexander 139
Power, Nelly 74-75
Price, Vincent 120
Primrose, Richard 77
Pullas (of Pullas and Cusick) 67
Pygmalion and his Gal(adear!) 44-45, 47, 92, 94

Queensberry (Marquess of) 75, 77

Rachel (of Rachel and Heloise) 41-42
Ralston (of Fish and Ralston) 85
Ramsden, Richard 30, 32-36, 38, 40, 68, 105
Raven, John 50
Redford (Captain, City of Richmond) 98-99, 101
Rice, Thomas Dartmouth 8
Richmond Sisters 85
Rickards, Carrie 30, 32
Rickards, Harry 30-33, 35, 38, 45, 47, 75, 78, 115-117
Riel, Louis 63-64
Riley, Mat 47
Robinson, Sir Hercules 34
Robinson, Lady 34

Rochfort, Mr 91
Rosenfeld, Sydney 90
Rossborough, HT 67
Rowe (of Rowe and Athol) 85
Royal Wild Beast Show, The 14
Russell, Lillian 128, 130
Ryland (of Sweeney and Ryland) 85

Saint-Saens, Charles-Camille, 13
Salsbury, Nate 85
Sami, Kami 38
Sarah Walker 34-35, 41
Saucy Flo 52
Saunders, Dan 147
Scott, Thomas 64
Seaward, William 70
Senator, The 90, 93, 96, 102, 104-105, 126
Sergeant Kitty 111, 112
Silent Sue 124
Silly Bill and Father 53
Simmonds, Henry 4
Simmonds (agents) 53
Sir Garnet Will Show Them The Way 62-64
Skeantlebury, Billy 53
Smollett, Tobias 139
Solomon, Edward 129-130
Something Like This 76
Spencer, 139
Spicer, Dr (Ship's Surgeon, St Vincent) 22
Steeplechase, The 57
Steinle, Max 108
St Felix Sisters 85
Sullivan, Sir Arthur 13